Public Opinion and Historians

Public Opinion and Historians

INTERDISCIPLINARY PERSPECTIVES

Edited by MELVIN SMALL

WAYNE STATE UNIVERSITY

WAYNE STATE UNIVERSITY PRESS / DETROIT / 1970

For Sara

Contents

Contents

Preface

As a historian interested in American opinion, I have made several excursions into that allegedly hostile realm of social science where I discovered a wealth of information, without which someone in my field could not intelligently sort out and explain his evidence. Yet, most historians are unaware of or uninterested in relevant research in sister disciplines. A cultural gap involving, among other things, the mysterious and convoluted jargon of the behavioral scientist frustrates interchange.

At the same time, apparently capable of understanding the less opaque language of the humanist, the behavioral scientist has been turning to the historian for data. While welcome, this development finds historians grinding out narrow, atheoretical monographs for other students of society. Obviously, the flow of theory, method, and data should run both ways—there is much the historian can and should borrow from his colleagues, who see him today as an unsophisticated data generator.

It was for these reasons that I decided to hold a symposium at which non-historians would display their wares in a specific field of concern to diplomatic, and tangentially, intellectual historians. In turn, historians would evaluate what these alien scholars had to offer. Thus, aside from my own introductory paper (which, to maintain symmetry, is discussed by a political scientist), the five formal papers were presented by three political scientists, a sociologist, and a professor of English, and the critiques by card-carrying historians. Each of the authors from the outside disciplines was asked to be as non-technical as possible in order to establish a common language with the humanist, and as the papers reveal, they succeeded in this first important prerequisite for a healthy dialogue.

Part I introduces the field, describes how and why historians have looked at public opinion, and then moves on to the relationship between social science and historians. Part II deals with theory as Paul F. Lazarsfeld examines the historian from the perspective of a sociologist, Bernard C. Cohen explains the weaknesses in the historian's model of the policy making process and public opinion, and Harold R. Isaacs suggests where the historian might look for sources of image or opinion. Part III revolves around a discussion of methodologies available to the student of opinion. Leo Marx presents the case for the intuitive approach of the American Studies scholars, and Richard L. Merritt offers a study of an empirical content analysis. Throughout, the discussants J. David Singer, Bradford Perkins, Alfred H. Kelly, Athan Theoharis, Edward Lurie, and John Higham weigh the merits of the papers in the light of their own research interests and experiences.

The Wayne State Fund generously provided the funds for the symposium, "Public Opinion, Foreign Policy, and the Historian," which was held at Wayne State University on May 8 and 9, 1967. In addition, the history department and graduate school of the University contributed various forms of financial assistance to aid in the completion of this project.

M. S.

Part One
INTRODUCTION

I

In this introductory chapter Melvin Small outlines the dimensions of the problems to be considered in this volume. A student of America's foreign relations, he is interested in the relationship between public opinion and the policy making process. Throughout this paper he calls attention to books and articles in the behavioral sciences that many historians have ignored.

J. David Singer, who discusses the paper, is the author of Deterrence, Arms Control, and Disarmament (1962) *and editor of* Quantitative International Politics (1968). *Singer has long advocated the use of behavioral methods in the study of international relations.*

Historians Look at
Public Opinion

◆

Melvin Small

DEPARTMENT OF HISTORY, WAYNE STATE UNIVERSITY

"Since public opinion is supposed to be the prime mover in democracies, one might reasonably expect to find a vast literature. One does not find it." So wrote Walter Lippmann in 1922, and his message has been heeded.[1] Today, a "vast literature" does exist, but unfortunately, most historians are unfamiliar with it. This would not be disastrous were it not the case that historians have written hundreds of monographs about the relationship between public opinion and historical events.[2] Because of their woeful ignorance of advances in related disciplines, their weighty tomes concerning opinions a public or publics in one society may have held about another public, institution, or society, all too often are intellectually barren.

I propose to examine the diplomatic historian's traditional approach to the study of public opinion, to suggest alternate research strategies, and to raise questions which will be dealt with in the succeeding papers. As I am interested primarily in America's foreign relations and recently have been concerned with American images of Germany during the Progressive Era, the bulk of this paper necessarily will involve problems encountered in my research.[3] Naturally, this emphasis on both American and diplomatic history limits the relevance of the discussion to follow.

In the first place, more than any other student of international relations, the American diplomatic historian must grapple with that terribly elusive concept, public opinion. In no other country has the general public played such a significant role in the determination of foreign policies. This factor presumably weakens any claims made about the universality of my approach. At the same time, public opinion becomes increasingly important in the late nineteenth and early twentieth centuries in the diplomacy of all the great powers to a point where Bismarck, Joseph Chamberlain, and Khrushchev had to worry almost as much about their publics as did Polk, McKinley, and Wilson.[4] Thus, while this paper relates to the American experience, most of it has relevance for the student of modern international relations.

Not that the problems to be discussed have no temporal limits. The historian of public, as distinct from elite, opinion is interested in those epochs when that opinion had some bearing on events. While it would be intriguing to know what the Russian serfs thought of Peter the Great's wars, the sources are not available. Moreover, the impact of serf opinion on Peter's decision making process was minimal. At the other end of the temporal continuum, because of the sophistication of polling techniques, the historian of recent diplomacy has a relatively simple and occasionally reliable tool for the study of opinion.[5] These factors necessarily restrict our interest to a period no longer than one hundred years for most countries —the eighteen forties to the nineteen forties. Of course, in terms of the communication and transportation revolutions, these one hundred years may be qualitatively equivalent to the previous five hundred. That is, there is more "history per square year" in the nineteenth century than the ninth.[6]

A second limitation also merits attention. Some historians, especially those interested in intellectual history and American Studies, have displayed a sensitivity to and awareness of both the problems in image studies and the existence of social science. Lamentably, the diplomatic historian, among the most conservative and unimaginative of his breed, is not included in this group.[7] This paper, therefore, is a critique of just one branch of the discipline.

After thus delineating the frame of reference, the student must verify the assumption that public opinion plays a role in the policy making process. No studies *prove* this traditional piece of folklore. On the other hand, few historians or political scientists challenge it, either on empirical or intuitive grounds. Until more work is done in this area, the scholar must practice a not very admirable form of intellectual obfuscation and point to legitimizers who have accepted the all important assumption.

Typical of political scientists are Richard Snyder and Edgar Furniss, who state in their influential text, "No nation in the world pays greater deference to something called public opinion than does the United States." The distinguished historian Dexter Perkins feels that "the general sentiment of the people lies at the root of every great issue." And the State Department itself periodically confirms that public opinion has much to do with its formulation of foreign policies.[8] But aside from a score of historical anecdotes, no one has been able to say very much more. Perhaps Bernard Cohen, who has spent the past year interviewing State Department officials, will shed some light on this matter. Of course, his conclusions may not be germane to the State Department of 1910 or 1880.

While little hard evidence exists about the allegedly intimate relationship between public opinion and policy maker, there is general agreement about the role opinion probably plays. That role, which varies from issue to issue, has been described as one which sets certain limits and goals for policy makers.[9] In other words, the public defines broad strategy, and the President and his aides define and execute tactics. At least this is one idealized portrayal of the relationship, but it never seems to work that simply all of the time. The debate over the bombing of North Vietnam, for example, can be interpreted as a debate over tactics; a concern, according to the model, beyond the legitimate purview of the public. It might well be that the role postulated above is the role the critics of the legendarily naive and uninformed public would like that public to play, and not necessarily the role it has played historically.

In any event, few would argue with the proposition that public opinion in the United States and most modern nations affects the policy making process, if not by initiating programs, by limiting options. After stating this, however, the student of public opinion is often cautioned not to under-emphasize the importance of the several official and non-official elites in shaping policy, and more significantly, in molding opinion.[10] But even historians have not ignored elites. What they have ignored, though, are the effects of elites on public opinion as well as the effects of factors more subtle than overt elite or governmental propaganda.[11]

One reason for this lacuna, aside from the fallacious one that elites have always been all important, is that it is easier to report elite opinion than public opinion, especially in pre-Gallup eras. To present the views of politicians, editors, and writers is far simpler than to make even educated guesses about the opinions of huge sections of that anonymous public which leaves behind no readily accessible letters, speeches, or editorials.[12]

For generations historians interested in public opinion have concentrated on elite opinion and confused the two.[13] In a respected monograph, which was considered relatively daring in its day, Charles Downer Hazen examined American opinions of the French Revolution. What Hazen really talks about were opinions of prominent Americans—opinions which *may* have reflected more general patterns of opinion.[14] The first half of this treatment of "American opinion" is devoted to the attitudes of three diplomats who manned the American legation in Paris during the Revolutionary years, Thomas Jefferson, James Monroe, and Gouverneur Morris. Although the second half is broader and includes congressional speeches, memoirs, and newspaper commentary, it still does not grapple with popular American views of the French Revolution.

Hazen most likely was unaware of the shortcomings of his approach. Establishing precedents for many later scholars, he fails to discuss the relationship between his findings and the policy making process and does not question or even make explicit his most general methodological assumptions. Moreover, his brand of scholarship is by no means an artifact of an unsophisticated age. In 1941 Andrew J. Torrieli published *Italian Opinion on America as Revealed by Italian Travelers, 1850–1900*. While the title is modest and perhaps accurate, Torrieli feels that his selection of travelers represents a cross section of late nineteenth century Italy. He concludes, therefore, that analysis of their memoirs can lead to "generalizations on the state of the Italian mind."[15] Nowhere does he demonstrate that his travelers come from all social, economic, and cultural levels of the Italian population. Again we find methodological confusion which results in the presentation of a welter of potentially useful yet ambiguous information.

It is not altogether surprising, then, that in 1931 Eber Malcolm Carroll, the diplomatic historian most closely associated with the study of public opinion, could begin his first major work with these words, "The historical development of public opinion in its relation to foreign affairs is a comparatively new field of investigation."[16] Considered revolutionary in his time, Carroll calls for the expansion of diplomatic history beyond the stultifying confines of treaties and secret negotiations. Ignoring studies that only recently had been completed in allied fields, the "pioneering"

Carroll explains his intention of using the newspaper editorial (the "most effective instrument for influencing public opinion and the most important medium for its expression") as his major tool for uncovering public opinion.[17] This approach, although more sophisticated than one which confuses elite with public opinion, is not without hazards far subtler than those that bedevil Hazen and his followers. Above all, Carroll, who also establishes many precedents, is unable to relate editorial opinion to public opinion. Even though he realizes the tenuous nature of his labors, and so warns his readers, he easily slides into gross oversimplifications. For example, he concludes on the basis of a series of editorials, *"The attention of public opinion* was concentrated almost exclusively upon domestic politics for more than a year before the July crisis of 1870."[18]

This class of error is rather common. In an article on the Portsmouth Peace Conference, one historian reports that his survey of fifty representative newspapers and periodicals made "clear that there was no shift of American opinion of the kind or degree claimed." In an even more glaring intellectual indiscretion he comments, "The decisive proof of Witte's failure to win American sympathy was the fact that the great majority of the press remained unswervingly pro-Japanese."[19] Similarly, the authors of a study of American opinion of Japan note that in 1907, "Everyone was relieved that the tension was over, but all were not satisfied with the solution. In the eastern part of the United States, the *New York Times,* the *Brooklyn Eagle* and the *New York World* . . ."[20] Even Thomas A. Bailey, a dean of American diplomatic historians and a public opinion specialist, is not immune. In his widely used text, on one occasion he implies that "the people" and the *Washington Post* are one and the same; on another occasion he offers, "But in general the rank and file of the American people were so little concerned with diplomacy that the *New York Sun* could declare in 1889 . . ."[21]

Perhaps the most carefully structured example of a traditional study is Meno Lovenstein's *American Opinion of Soviet Russia.* Lovenstein, who does not rely on newspapers alone, presents a body of evidence which he suggests shaped American views of Russia from 1917 to 1933. He divides his period into three time spans—1917–21, 1921–29, 1929–33—and within each of these areas methodically offers samplings of opinions and types of coverage from business and financial magazines, trade papers, economic journals, labor journals, learned journals, general magazines, books, newspapers, and government documents. As he implies in his conclusion, Lovenstein is interested less in public opinion than in the honest and complete portrayal of the Soviet Union by the public media.[22] Consequently, a more accurate if clumsy title for this study would be "The Attention and Care Given to the Soviet Union in Selected Magazines, Books, and Newspapers." This unwillingness to use qualifying or explanatory phrases, such as "opinion, *as expressed in American newspapers*," or "the people, *who may have agreed with the New York Times when it stated editorially*," leads many historians into intellectually careless practices. And even these unesthetic constructions would probably not legitimize the inherent methodological assumptions.

In the last analysis, what have passed for studies of mass opinion, often have been elaborate examinations of newspaper and magazine editorials. Historians have continually confused editorial opinion with public opinion, despite the fact that social scientists several decades ago clarified the relationship. In the first article of the first issue of *Public Opinion Quarterly* in 1937, Floyd H. Allport sets forth the credo of the public opinion analyst. Among the common fallacies in the field, he includes the "journalistic fallacy" of labeling editorials as public opinion, or "the confusion of public opinion with the public presentation of opinion," a "naive error." [23]

Allport's critique has been substantiated in part by scholars who have examined the relationship between editorial and public opinion in American life. Using presidential election returns as their dependent variables, both Elmo Wilson and Frank Luther Mott fail to discover meaningful correlations between editorial and public opinion. In addition, after studying Seattle newspapers, George A. Lundberg concludes that their editorial policies had little influence on given issues, and above all, readers did not purchase papers because of specific biases manifested in news or editorial columns.[24]

Others note that editorials, which allegedly influence as well as reflect public opinion, are not read by the majority of readers. Valdimer Orlando Key explains that different readers concentrate on different sections of different magazines and newspapers. Common sense indicates that sports news and comic pages are read as much as, if not more than, less frivolous sections of a paper.[25]

Of course, the historian of mid-nineteenth century American opinion should pay careful attention to the newspaper editorial. While the editorial may never have reflected opinion, it may have influenced it from the eighteen sixties to the eighteen eighties, the heyday of personal journalism. Here, and only here, were American papers noted for their editorial pages. After this brief period, personal journalism declines in significance to a point where editorials are among the last items read, if they are read at all.[26]

Nevertheless, although the editorial is not a very important vehicle for influencing or reflecting public opinion in normal times, the situation could change during crises or periods of supposed heightened interest in foreign affairs when citizens are eager for information and guidance.[27] Yet, even during such times, it is debatable whether Americans are affected any differently by news media. During a crucial phase of the Korean War, Alfred O. Hero found roughly twenty-five percent of the American population not even interested in what was going on in the most general sense; and during normal periods, he depicts apathy and indifference to world affairs as characteristics of half the population.[28] If this is the situation today, one can imagine the lack of interest in diplomacy during those halcyon days of isolation and security before Sarajevo.

In fact, in prewar America newspapers joined the public in displaying little interest in the world. Except for a few major dailies, coverage of *Weltpolitik* was so sketchy that historians cannot hope to discover Progressive America's opinion of Europe from editorial pages, and this goes for hemispheric problems as well. During 1905, a year which saw a bitter conflict over the Dominican Republic protectorate treaty and the establishment of that pilot project for the Roosevelt Corollary, the *New York Times,* the most cosmopolitan of American papers, offered a total of thirty-odd items on the affair.[29] American diplomat Joseph C. Grew wrote from Berlin in 1912 about the inadequate coverage of key foreign developments in American newspapers, "I have almost given up reading them now for even the best of them are filled with page after page of murder and suicide accounts, while the most important political matters of world interest are given short paragraphs and sandwiched in where one can scarcely find them."[30]

Aware of many of these criticisms of his technique, the historian stubbornly insists on relying upon the same tired tools of public opinion evaluation and still equates editorials in the *New York Times* of 1908 with public opinion on the Bosnian crisis! There is, however, a compelling defense for the traditional methodology, at least as it relates to the policy maker's perception of public opinion. In his discussion of French public opinion in the Third Republic, Eber Malcolm Carroll emphasizes the impact of various editorials on the Quai d'Orsay and is able to produce evidence to support his contention that French statesmen looked for public opinion in the press. More recently, Bernard C. Cohen found that State Department officials in the mid-fifties also identified editorials with public opinion.[31]

If Carroll and Cohen are correct, and there is little reason to doubt their findings, then the question of public opinion, the editorial, and their relationship to policy becomes more complex. Is public opinion what the general populace thought at a given time, or is it what a user of public opinion, the diplomat, thought it to be? If the contemporary policy maker considers editorials his most accurate reflection of public opinion, then the historian who does little more than collate editorials is presenting a valid expression of opinion which shaped events.

An acceptance of this argument devalues the significance of the search for opinion beyond the newspaper, especially if the subject is studied to learn about the policy making process. This would certainly be the case if other scholars' findings for other countries and other eras replicate those of Carroll and Cohen.

Be that as it may, the search for opinion as it really was is still a useful endeavor. The problem is similar to the one involving German penetration of Latin America before World War I. German archival materials reveal that the Wilhelmstrasse had no serious designs on bases near the Panama Canal. The fact that Americans *thought* they did remains of great importance, nonetheless, and thus a complete study must be made of both the realities and what were thought to be the realities during the period.

In any event, the historian cannot facilely equate editorial opinion with public opinion. When he deals with opinion expressed publicly in a newspaper, he must label it as such and use it as merely one indicator among many of public opinion. The specific significance of the editorial as either influencer or reflector of opinion most likely would depend upon the nature of the culture or the era in which it is written and read.

Despite reservations about the newspaper as the major source in opinion studies, it does play a role in defining issues about which publics develop opinions, or as Bernard Cohen tells us, it may not "be successful in telling people what to think, but it is . . . in telling its readers what to think *about*."[32] Indeed, during the period of our chief concern, a period which predates radio, television, and motion pictures, the newspaper was the sole reading material for ninety percent of the population. This dominance continued at least until 1950, when the paper still was read more widely than magazines or books.[33] Consequently, the newspaper cannot be ignored, for it generally defines the relative importance of historical events for its readers.

All too often historians impose their value systems upon an age that saw things from different perspectives. The result of this process, which usually involves a careless examination of the press, is a distortion of the impact of "news" during the period in question.[34] For example, Progressive America should have been "buzzing" about the Kaiser's *London Daily Telegraph* interview of October 1908. This dramatic story did receive a good deal of attention but not nearly as much as might be expected. The reason for this seeming lack of worldliness or proportion does not necessarily lie in the insularity of the United States, but in the fact that Americans were "buzzing" about their presidential election when the German story broke. In those pre-computer days, several weeks went by before all the state returns finally trickled into Washington. Thus, each day's lead story most often involved a new election result. These accounts of the deposition of a senator here and the loss of a legislature there overshadowed, both in terms of attention and page placement, reports of the tottering of the Hohenzollern Empire. A comparable situation occurred in October 1964 when, in less than forty-eight hours, the Chinese exploded an atomic device, Khrushchev resigned, and the pennant-winning New York Yankees fired their manager. Had each of these stories appeared separately, they would have received far more attention than they did at the time. Thirty years from now, any historian who tries to assess American opinion of the first Chinese nuclear explosion must employ the press to evaluate the country's information overload.

Moreover, examination of contemporary newspapers often reveals forgotten stories which once rocked an age. In that year of the regal interview, a report appeared in American media which, judging by the copy expended on it, caused more excitement in German-American relations than any story from Manila Bay to Sarajevo. Kaiser Wilhelm announced rather indiscreetly (as was his wont) that the new American ambassador, who had been cleared by the Wilhelmstrasse, was unacceptable to him. The story and the furor surrounding it have all but disappeared from standard histories, yet anyone evaluating American opinion of Germany before World War I would discover that this obscure incident had a greater impact than the Agadir or Zabern affairs.

Obviously, the historian of opinion cannot discard the newspaper, but he can begin supplementing it with a wider variety of sources. And here he might be aided conceptually by a redefinition of terms. "Opinion" is a narrow term compared to "image," for opinions are "verbal answers that an individual gives in response to stimulus situations" in which some question is asked; they are issue oriented or expressions "on a controversial point of view."[35] As long as we are dealing with editorials, the use of the term "opinion" is in order, for the editorial easily meets definitional requirements. But editorials are opinions of newspapermen stated publicly, and if we are after *public* opinion, the term is clearly inappropriate. Moreover, since it is unlikely that we can discern public opinion in pre-Gallup eras, we are interested in more unconscious, broader, non-verbalized "images."[36] "Images" can be defined as a man's "subjective knowledge of the world," which includes all his "beliefs, attitudes, information, preferences," or "pictures in the head."[37]

This is where the diplomatic historian may offer the rejoinder that we know little about the formation of images in today's world, let alone the world of Theodore Roosevelt. Nevertheless, the mere fact that one deals with such relatively ethereal concepts as images, for which no solid data exist comparable to treaties or government documents, is not a sufficient reason to abandon potentially useful but unorthodox sources and methods. This will involve entering the realm of the imponderable, but it is better to enter it, however cautiously, than to throw up one's hands at its many ambiguities.

Happily, agreement exists among social scientists on the general nature of images. Few would dispute the propositions that images are simpler than reality, often contradictory, difficult to change, and most important, images of foreigners are usually negative to some degree.[38] While these latter include stark residues of former wars and diplomatic

crises, they are composed, in the main, of more intangible "pictures."
Walter Lippmann wrote:

> When we use the word "Mexico" what picture does it evoke in a resident of
> New York? Likely as not, it is some composite of sand, cactus, and wells,
> greasers, rum-drinking Indians, testy old cavaliers flourishing whiskers and
> sovereignty, or perhaps an idyllic peasantry à la Jean Jacques, assailed by the
> prospect of smoky industrialism, and fighting for the Rights of Man.

Lippmann also asks about the image of Japan: "Is it a vague horde of
slant-eyed yellow men, surrounded by Yellow Perils, picture brides . . .
Samurai, banzais, art and cherry blossoms?"[39] Writing in 1921, he does
not mention Carranza or Pancho Villa, Yap or Shantung, but concen-
trates on images evoked by popular stories and myths.

At this moment the editors of the *New York Times,* the *Washington
Post,* and the *Christian Science Monitor* may be writing editorials about
an impending clash with Switzerland over tariff policies. Two days from
now, both nations might break diplomatic relations and thus precipitate a
minor crisis which would make the front pages of all the newspapers. The
public, looking at the word "Switzerland" in headlines, would not think
of the earlier editorials in prestige papers that denounced the greedy Swiss
(which of course it had not read).[40] Instead, it immediately would think
of a pleasant land of snow, chalets, skis, neutrality, chocolate, and hardy
democrats. When and if the American government planned further
action against the Swiss in this hypothetical confrontation, it would have
to take into account the public mood towards Switzerland, a mood
conditioned by favorable images and devoid of the hostility towards the
little country shared by American watchmakers and editorial writers. The
historian of this Swiss-American crisis (and some young scholar would be
writing a thesis about it around 1980) could not rely on editorials which
appeared in newspapers two days before the crisis for an accurate picture
of the American image of Switzerland in the Spring of 1967. It would
stand to reason, then, that if one wanted to study American images of the
protagonists in World War I in the summer of 1914, he would look
beyond newspaper editorials on *Weltpolitik.* Unfortunately, this has not
been done.

Diplomatic historians must assume that publics of any epoch construct images of foreign countries from an infinite variety of sources, some presently available, many not. Mark Sullivan, a careful observer of the American scene, concludes in *Our Times* that Americans probably had a favorable image of Germany on the eve of Sarajevo. He attributes this image, in large measure, to German-Americans in thousands of cities and villages across the country—friendly, patriotic citizens who enriched national life with beer, music and gesundheit![41] To measure quantitatively or evaluate intuitively Sullivan's purveyors of image would be difficult if not impossible, especially since there is no way to poll citizens of an earlier age. Yet it may well be that the journalist's impressionistic items were the most important sources for images of Germany.

One factor might ameliorate this frustrating situation to a limited degree. Since mass publics generally develop vague and inconsistent images about foreign countries, they are easily influenced by printed materials arguing specific points. That is, the more uninformed a person is about foreign policy and the more his images are unrelated to *Weltpolitik,* the more susceptible he is to "authoritative" newspaper or magazine features.[42]

Despite this tenuous argument, the student of image can only present part of the story, and generally that part having to do with public media. And because of the awesome inferential gap between purveyors of images and readers' images, the most he can do is evaluate varieties of printed materials which contributed to those images. Unless one is concerned exclusively with elites or the history of intellectuals, he cannot equate images in books and magazines with popular images. The task of merely presenting material *likely* to affect images is a narrow and relatively unexciting one, but the honest historian can do little more.

After conceding that only some of the bones are left for the historian to pick over, a scheme for handling printed materials contributing to images of foreign countries must be devised. The two classes of problems in this realm relate to the sampling of materials and the methodologies available for their evaluation. After discussing these admittedly difficult problems, the historian might beat a hasty retreat to the safe confines of the newspaper.

Above all, he must recognize that all books, magazines, and newspapers containing references to another country or culture are probable sources for images. For example, to study contemporary American images of Switzerland, one must look not only at the *Times, Foreign Affairs,* and scholarly treatises on "Switzerland, the United States, and the Balance of Power," but at images in textbooks, novels, travel guides, popular and specialized magazines, songs, billboards and advertisements, radio, television, theatres, motion pictures, sermons, and polls. Given our temporal limitations, our primary interest will center on printed materials.[43]

Beginning with books, most important in terms of circulation and impact are schoolbooks. Meticulously read by more citizens than the Bible, grammars, spellers, and readers present general images of foreign cultures which are likely to stick with the child through the rest of his adult life.[44] Images of wooden shoes, igloos, and chopsticks readily come to mind. Here, stress should be placed on the most widely used elementary readers, like the fabled McGuffey series, rather than on specialized histories or geographies. In 1918, for instance, the former American ambassador to Germany complained about a speller used in all Chicago city schools which contained only one piece of reading matter, "a fulsome eulogy of the present German Emperor."[45] In addition, considering patterns of school attendance and literacy, grammar school books should be weighted more heavily than intermediate or high school texts.

Next in significance, probably, are pulp fiction, dime novels, and other literarily undistinguished but cheap best-selling works, which unfortunately are not collected by most libraries. These, along with comic books and fan magazines, are either non-existent or unavailable for earlier periods. Whenever rich sources like the Horatio Alger series are available, however, they must be read.

More sophisticated popular novels become increasingly important in the twentieth century with its mass reading public. Indeed, novels which appear as apolitical entertainment or art often affect national images more than Council on Foreign Relations volumes devoted explicitly to diplomacy. In other words, constant exposure to the dull but honest German burgher who appears in generations of American novels eventually might convince readers that all Germans are dull and honest.[46]

The main problem with the diplomatic historian's use of the novel is that he usually asks a specific question about one country's image of another over a limited period of time. If the historian is searching for clues to the general intellectual climate of an age, then a close examination of novels is mandatory, but the student of international relations seldom is interested in so broad a subject.[47] In many cases the analysis of novels for images of foreign countries becomes a luxury in terms of time and magnitude of payoff. I once tried to discern images of Germany presented to American readers in novels of the Progressive Era. Sixteen novels ranging from *Pollyanna* to *The House of Mirth* were read word by word with discouraging results. Coders found very few references to Germany, German characters, or German culture, and those they did find were often vague and devoid of values.[48] This is not to say that all students of image should ignore novels. Certainly, any examination of American images of China would have to include a discussion of Pearl S. Buck, but it is only necessary to deal with best sellers which explicitly cover the country of interest.

The last category of books is popular non-fiction. Compared to novels, they usually do not enjoy a wide circulation, and many which are sold often are not read. In twentieth century middle class society, "readers" purchase such weighty tomes as *Understanding Media* so that they can place them prominently on coffee tables to demonstrate their worldliness to visitors. Nevertheless, books on diplomacy and world politics, history, government, and biography should all be scrutinized.[49] Less scholarly books, interestingly, may be even more influential. Travel guides have rarely been examined by historians, even though physical images often are the basic images of foreign countries. Thus, in the years before World War I, the Germany of romantic Rothenburg and Bavarian forests depicted in popular travel books made that country among the first to be visited in any real or imagined grand tour.

If discussion of varieties of books opens a Pandora's box of problems, the situation is even worse with magazines, where the student is virtually inundated with materials ranging from mass circulation weeklies to specialized journals. Again, one is interested in articles on theatre and school systems as well as those on battleships and imperialism. The historian of American images of England from 1930 to 1940 must look at both an article on India in *Foreign Affairs* and the sensational story of the abdication in *Cosmopolitan*.

With the magazine, sampling procedures cause the greatest difficulties. If the scholar is seeking images of a crisis, as often is the case, his temporal limits are circumscribed. To discover press reactions to the two-week Cuban missile crisis in magazines, he conceivably could read all the magazines which discussed it. If he is studying images of a country over a longer period of time, however, he runs into trouble. While it is possible to limit arbitrarily the magazine phase of the research to all pertinent entries in the *Readers' Guide,* even here the task could be burdensome, especially if one had to analyze all references to Germany from 1930 to 1940. The situation becomes more desperate if the survey of magazines is only part of a larger survey of all media. Moreover, when he restricts himself to the *Readers' Guide,* the historian ignores many local periodicals often rather meaningful in shaping images. It is altogether likely that farmers in Wisconsin in 1914 were more influenced by the *Wisconsin Agriculturist* than they were by *Collier's.*[50] On the other hand, once beyond the *Readers' Guide,* where does one stop?

Then again, the problem of manageability raises its pernicious head in the treatment of magazine fiction as opposed to non-fiction. If the decision is made to explore the sentimental world of magazine fiction and stories in the *Saturday Evening Post* and the *Ladies' Home Journal* are examined, then logically, so too should the contents of often ephemeral mass magazines of the *True Story–True Romance* genre.[51]

Or at the extreme opposite end of the spectrum, every year hundreds of national and local historical and scholarly journals publish articles about the history and life of various nations. Does the student of images have the time to go into *Michigan History* as well as the *American Historical Review,* and is there anything to be gained by evaluating a commentary on Frederick the Great or Tacitus?

Moving to a different medium, one should examine the popular play, or more exactly, scripts of plays performed during the period under surveillance. Old theatrical presentations are comparable to motion pictures in terms of impact on the audience, and we know that motion pictures and television today are more powerful purveyors of images than printed materials. Here one would be interested in plays which were seen by the largest audiences rather than those which were merely artistically distinguished. Obviously a Jerry Lewis "comedy" affects more people than a Truffaut film. Stock characters of immigrant types presented over and over in the American theatre helped shape images of Germany, Ireland, Italy, and other countries. The printed script, of course, is a poor substitute for the live performance.

Finally, in terms of sources other than the ubiquitous newspaper, there is the popular song. While the song, like the play, does not quite belong with printed purveyors of images as far as the historian is concerned, the melody may not linger on but the score often does. Who is to say that American images of the Irish were not molded by the wealth of songs about the beautiful Emerald Isle and her happy, romantic people?

Although this list of sources for images of foreign countries is still far from exhaustive, it does go beyond that traditional source, the editorial. The weighty problems of sampling have not been settled as they obviously relate to the peculiarities of each distinct research proposal.

Given this broad definition of available sources, a student of the American image of England from 1900 to 1920 would need to look at virtually everything published during the period—a formidable assignment. Although a sensible sampling scheme is a priority of the first order, it cannot be drawn up until the more important problems of data analysis are solved.

Beginning with the most rudimentary problem, since the student of popular images is not as concerned with *opinions* of writers of books and articles as he is with their *impact,* he has to assume the stories he evaluates were read by purchasers. Here he is treading on thin ice for, as we have seen with the newspaper, not everyone reads all of what he buys. Consequently, many more readers of the *Saturday Evening Post* were drawn to an A. B. Guthrie "Western" than to a feature on NATO. Because of the lack of data in this area for periods prior to the thirties, the historian cannot determine whether the piece he is evaluating was ever read.[52]

A far more critical problem concerns the evaluation of a source in terms of the impression it left on the contemporary reader—the attempt to simulate mental patterns and value systems of a majority of readers of a bygone age. What strikes today's scholar as a favorable image, might have struck the contemporary reader as an unfavorable one. A story in a 1912 *Collier's,* which praised the German army as a universal training school for good citizenship and a boon to national health, might have been accompanied by photographs of huge cannon and men girded for war. This article, favorable in intent, could reenforce stereotypes of spike-helmeted militarists, the images conveyed in the pictures, and just those images the author attempted to dispel in his copy.[53] Or similarly, a story which attacked Jewish control of finance in an otherwise happy country in Central Europe in 1910 might not have been taken the same way by a contemporary reader as it is by a scholar sensitive to anti-Semitism.

A partial solution is empirical content analysis, a tool generally ignored by historians.[54] One reason for this (being charitable and assuming there are intellectual as well as emotional objections to "counting") may be that their problems are usually broader than those who have employed the tool on historical data in other disciplines. For example, when Ithiel de Sola Pool and his group studied newspaper attention and biases towards international relations, his coding rules were comparatively simple, entailing the classification and counting of words and groups of words in editorials in leading establishment papers for selected periods of time.[55] In like manner, Richard L. Merritt defined a narrow, manageable task for himself in looking for changes in terminology for the North American colonies in American colonial newspapers for a few decades before the Revolution to find at what point the press began to refer to their country with a term which distinguished it from England.[56]

Suppose the content analyst has to report on American images of Germany as evidenced in American media from 1900 to 1920. Using a content analytic methodology, he now must not only count words and phrases relating to a handful of concepts in editorials, but he must also be concerned with a multiplicity of variables—placement, type face, length of articles, continuations beyond page one and their content and placement, photographs, and so on.[57] Then, of course, the circulations of various journals as well as the quality of their readerships are additional inputs. Especially perplexing in terms of establishing valid coding rules are problems relating to distinctions between straight news and features. What rules can be devised to distinguish between an objective account of an unpleasant event, such as the signing of the Nazi-Soviet pact, and a feature column opposing the pact? Is not the editorial attack, for most American readers in 1939, redundant and obvious? To be sure, all of these distinctions can be weighted, but many of the coding rules will be arbitrary, such as the assignment to all lead stories on page one twice the weight of material on the bottom of page two.[58] The continual "plugging in" of new weighting rules places the validity of the entire scheme in jeopardy. Yet, something must be done. Surely an unfavorable reference to the British theatre on page thirty-seven of the *Times* has a different impact than an editorial critical of Rhodesia in that same august paper.

A related problem involves the audiences and their relative influence in society. Would a favorable piece in the low-circulation *Nation* balance an unfavorable one in *Reader's Digest?* How many masses equal one elite? One way out of this dilemma makes use of the theories of Elihu Katz and Paul F. Lazarsfeld on the "two step flow of communication" which sees opinion leaders transmitting images they pick up in their media to the rest of the community.[59] Thus, the historian need only concern himself with magazines read by "influentials," and therefore, the article in *Nation* is more important in shaping national images than is the feature in *Reader's Digest.* Unfortunately, this approach poses both methodological and theoretical difficulties. In the first place, how does one find opinion makers and their reading material in American communities of 1890? Secondly, some social scientists disagree with aspects of the Katz-Lazarsfeld model. Philip E. Converse, for one, finds a wide gap between the belief systems of elites and the general public.[60]

And even if we solved the problems of defining audiences and establishing an acceptable scheme of content analysis, could we say any more than x amount of y type of symbols were read by x number of z class people? Content analysis cannot tell us about the specific effect or impact of articles or books even if we know who is reading them.[61]

Problems of effect measurement are further encountered in the weighting of different categories of printed materials. Straight news stories in which biases intrude subtly often are more potent shapers of image than editorial opinion labeled as such. When a reader perceives that someone is trying to persuade him to adopt a certain position, that persuader appears to have something to gain and thus the reader does not trust him.[62] In other words, a scathing editorial on Gamal Abdul Nasser may not be as influential as an Associated Press dispatch which uses the phrase "the Egyptian dictator" in its seemingly neutral account. At the same time, experimenters talk of a "sleeper effect" which finds the initially skeptical reader of an editorial opinion influenced by that same opinion several weeks later when he forgets where he read it.[63]

Even more challenging is the question of image retention over time. If the historian is concerned with a period of crisis, he usually looks back over the preceding decade or so for materials which conditioned reactions during that crisis. German-American relations immediately before World War I were marked by two confrontations, the Manila Bay affair of 1898 and the Venezuela incident of 1902-03. Both of these were dramatic crises involving the clash of rival imperialisms and both led to scores of reports about the probability of war between the two young giants. From 1903 on, though, official relations between the two potential antagonists were placid, and thus more and more observers began to increase the odds for German-American conflict. When war broke out in 1914, did Americans remember more clearly Manila Bay or the warm paeans to Wilhelm II which appeared in all media to honor his Silver Jubilee in 1913?

As in comparable areas in opinion or image research, social scientists are themselves unsure of the answer. Some report that people stubbornly cling to images unless a very dramatic event intervenes, and even then, old images persist.[64] This finding leads to the conclusion that no matter what may have happened from 1903 to 1914, the absence of very dramatic events meant that on the eve of the war, Americans still thought of the Manila Bay outrage whenever they thought of Germany. If this is true, how long would it have taken for those images to recede—another ten years? Several generations?

On the other hand, Americans are notoriously fickle and unpredictable in their vacillations of national mood, as can be seen in their rapid change of opinion of Russia and Germany from 1945 to 1949.[65] Whichever approach is correct, and both are to some degree, the historian is faced with the vexing problem of evaluating the impact of events which may have taken place ten or twenty years before his period of major concern.

Finally, even if a historian solves most of his difficulties, and concludes that during a certain era Americans thought favorably or unfavorably about another country, he still has not completed his task. Suppose, for example, he demonstrates that Americans of the Progressive Era liked Germany. By itself, this conclusion is mildly interesting, but it reveals little about the potential impact of this public attitude on the policy making process. What is important is the relative position of Germany on an attitude scale including the other major powers.[66] Any historian who posits that Americans liked Germany and therefore did not like England is leaving himself open to a revisionist attack which would find that while Americans liked Germany, they loved England.

Other issues remain to be discussed, but lurking in the background is the most frustrating one of all for the historian interested in employing social science insights in his research—the enigmatic relationship between experiments and surveys in the 1950s and audiences of 1910. In much of the material cited above, contemporary sociologists and psychologists tested theories of opinion change, media preference, and reading habits with either small groups or surveys. Knowing this, can the historian of the Progressive Era borrow Deutsch and Merritt's theories about the effects of events on images when other scholars dispute the representativeness of their sample as well as the validity of their research technique? Even more distressing is the lack of correlation between survey and experimental data.[67]

At the same time, as consensuses (hopefully) develop around bodies of behavioral theory, the historian will be on more solid ground when he uses them for different epochs and publics. Then the last major stumbling block would be the fabled uniqueness of historical events, and here the historian can be criticised, for he has always compared events and sought intuitive generalizations about national as well as group behavior. If the historian can conclude that the Mexican War, the Spanish-American War, and World War I, reveal the crusading nature of American populations in wartime, then he should be able to accept the not completely unrelated proposition that if groups in the nineteen thirties, forties, and fifties, in forty different situations, were more affected by exposure to pictures than print, then Americans of 1910 probably reacted in a like manner. In most cases the historian easily accepts the first proposition but rejects the second. Hopefully, this volume will help break down some of the historian-erected barriers which have led to a rejection of social science research and methodologies.

Comment I

◆

J. David Singer

DEPARTMENT OF POLITICAL SCIENCE, UNIVERSITY OF MICHIGAN

THERE SEEM TO BE two alternative responses one can make to the paper which opens this volume. One option is to take up several of the important theoretical and substantive issues which are raised. The other is to focus on the equally critical issues of an epistemological nature which are raised, albeit in a less direct fashion. Given the brief space allotted me, it may seem foolish, but let me try to pick up a few ideas in each of these categories.

On the substantive side, even though we have made considerable progress in the observation and measurement of public opinion, we still have only the foggiest notion of (a) the factors that shape and change that opinion, and (b) the ways in which that opinion in turn shapes a nation's foreign policy. Let me suggest here the briefest sketch of a scheme that might help us move from a mere description of public opinion to an understanding of it as both an independent and a dependent variable.

Any single citizen's opinion on a given foreign policy problem at a given moment—if he has an opinion at all—is a consequence of some or all of the items in the following partial list: (a) his basic personality, (b) his general attitude toward the people and place and type of problem involved, (c) his level of information, (d) the credibility he assigns to the political leaders and media from whom he gets his information, (e) his status in the family, work group, and neighborhood, (f) his beliefs as to what "everyone else" thinks, (g) his mood at the time that the opinion is expressed, (h) whom he talked to most recently, and (i) the age, sex, style, and tone of the interviewer, if that is the way in which the opinion was ascertained. That opinion is also shaped by recent or remembered foreign policy *events,* or more accurately, the way in which those events are interpreted for him or by him.

Those same events are, of course, also shaped to some extent by the opinions of this man and his fellow citizens. A check list of those other factors that also help shape foreign policy events—and the specific behavior of a single nation—would certainly include: (a) the nation's basic capabilities vis-a-vis others, (b) the way in which its short- and middle-run objectives have been defined, and (c) the general structure of the international system at the time. In addition, and of immediate concern here, would be three further variables: (d) the extent to which the decision makers feel constrained to respond to public opinion, (e) the degree to which they believe that opinion might be manipulated, and (f) what might be termed the diplomatic culture of the period.

This final variable is most crucial, inasmuch as it embraces not only the national, regional, and global distribution of mass and elite opinions regarding the policy problem of the moment, but a far broader range of views. This cultural dimension also embraces the distribution of more general views or attitudinal configurations of three types: how nations *do* behave at the moment, how they *should* behave now and in the future, and how they *might* behave in the future. My point is that the kinds of modes, norms, and expectations we find at different levels of influence in the system as a whole will indeed create constraints and establish incentives for individual sets of decision makers in specific policy settings. And every foreign policy response to these domestic and global cultural phenomena will have some effect on which attitudes will be strengthened, weakened, or modified.

The theme I want to stress here, then, is that opinion and attitude (combining into something akin to "image," as used in Small's paper) may be thought of as a most critical link in the diplomatic feedback cycle. With opinions and attitudes influencing policy, and policy influencing these psychological factors in turn, no serious effort to understand global politics in general or a particular sequence of diplomatic events in particular can afford to ignore them. The problem before us next, of course, is to ascertain how much of the variance they account for in different types of cases, the degree to which that potency has been changing over time, and the extent to which they exercise a different effect in different types of national governments. Simultaneously, we must get on with an examination of the way in which the culture of the international system has been and is itself being affected by the day-to-day and year-to-year decisions of those who act, intelligently or otherwise, on behalf of their publics.

We cannot, however, make much progress toward an understanding of the culture-behavior–culture-feedback loop if we insist on stumbling along with the primitive research methods of history and traditional political science. While there is, in my judgment, considerable room for improvement in all phases of research on international politics, there is one phase that is of primary importance, and I should like to dwell on that in my remaining remarks. In general, all social science research can be divided into data-collection and data-analysis; we collect data in order to *describe* some event or situation, and we analyze data in order to *explain* it. Quite clearly, any effort to explain becomes a farce unless we have first rendered a satisfactory description of what we seek to explain.

As a political scientist who has worked closely with historians and their writings, I must in all honesty report that—with few exceptions—the descriptive methods used are sadly inadequate. The key weakness is the lack of what social scientists call "operational" description, by which we mean that the criteria by which one observes, measures, and describes must be made visible and explicit. As long as events are described and grouped by criteria which the reader may only guess at, and which may even remain vague or unknown to the writer himself, we have not even begun to make our work comparative and cumulative. I recognize, of course, there still are historians who believe that no two events or situations are similar and that each must therefore be treated in terms appropriate to its distinctive peculiarities, with neither comparison nor cumulative generalization a legitimate activity.

Two reservations come immediately to mind. First, we will never know *how* similar or dissimilar they are unless they are described in terms which at least permit comparability. Neither similarity nor dissimilarity can ever be assumed; it must always be an empirical question, to be answered only after we examine the evidence. Second, and closely related, is the fact that just about every word we use in diplomatic history implies, by definition, *some* degree of similarity. How can we speak of embargo, war, embassy, political party, or foreign ministry unless we believe that the word embraces a *class* of phenomena rather than a never-to-be-duplicated state of affairs of complete and total distinctiveness? If we want to differentiate among wars or foreign ministers for example, all well and good, but let us then operationally define the particular sub-classes, making explicit the criteria by which each case is assigned to a particular sub-class. There will, of course, be those who insist that there are as many sub-classes as there are specific cases, and all we can do then is let them go their own benighted way.

In sum, in his opening paper our host has made a strong move toward the development of a fuller understanding of public opinion and international diplomacy. He has turned to the behavioral sciences and has borrowed judiciously of their *findings* and *concepts*. This is a promising sign indeed, and when we begin to utilize their *methods* as well, we can safely say that diplomatic history and international politics have joined together to build a body of cumulative knowledge.

Part Two
THEORY

2

For several generations sociologists have studied public opinion, mass media, theories of organization, and a host of other subjects of interest to historians. While sharing these mutual concerns, sociologists have turned to historians for data far more frequently than historians have turned to sociologists for theoretical insight. In the main, historians have been unaware of or have chosen to ignore relevant research in this allied discipline.

Paul F. Lazarsfeld attempts to remedy this situation in this paper. Since his emigration to the United States in the late nineteen thirties, he has been among the most significant figures in the study of public opinion. Co-author of Personal Influence (1955) and The People's Choice (1944), he here discusses recent projects in sociology that the historian might find useful.

Bradford Perkins, who analyzes Lazarsfeld's suggestions, specializes in American diplomatic history. In his prize-winning Castlereagh and Adams (1964), the final volume of a trilogy on Anglo-American relations from 1795 to 1823, Perkins dealt with questions concerning public opinion and cross-cultural influences.

A Sociologist Looks
At Historians

◆

Paul F. Lazarsfeld

DEPARTMENT OF SOCIOLOGY, COLUMBIA UNIVERSITY

I DO NOT INTEND in the present remarks to discuss what the relation between history and sociology should or could be. Rather, I want to review some sociological work which in recent years seems to have had an influence on historical writings. In the end, I will turn around and describe some debts we sociologists owe to historians. I might as well begin with such an acknowledgement.

In the spirit of this gathering, a good part of my presentation will deal with research on public opinion. Until recently I might have forced myself to start with the meaning of such terms as "opinion" as compared to "attitude" or "disposition to act." Fortunately, a historian has saved me the necessity of such efforts. Donald Fleming has recently published an illuminating essay on the history of the attitude concept.[1] He shows how much this notion has changed since it first came into use about a hundred years ago. It has lost its connection with its physiological origin, and today combines a balance of two elements: a rational way and an emotional way of perceiving the outside world. "Stereotypes," "prejudices," and "opinions" are all special cases of attitudes, but with varying mixtures of the rational and emotional elements.

A first theme to discuss, then, is the contribution to historiography made by the study and analysis of attitudes. Three aspects of such work can be traced: (a) attitudes become quantifiable properties of people, as their age or their income; (b) this incorporates them into the language of social research, which permits us to talk in clear-cut propositions relating such characteristics to each other; (c) the analysis of such empirical

39

relations becomes a special skill which gives more precise meaning to such notions as "interpretation" and "cause." Let us begin with (b), the aspect of clarity. At the beginning of the century the German historian Hermann Oncken wrote an essay, "The Historian, the Statesman, and Public Opinion." I want to quote and discuss one passage from this essay (the inserted numbers will aid in the subsequent discussion).

> The vague and fluctuating cannot be understood by being clamped into a formula; certainly not when it is a very characteristic of the concept that it embodies a thousand possibilities of variation. But when all is said and done, everyone knows, if put to it, what public opinion means. If it must be set in words, then it can only appear hedged around by many restricting clauses: public opinion is a complex of similar utterances of larger or smaller segments of society concerning public affairs (1, 2); at times spontaneous, at times artfully manipulated (3); expressed in a multitude of ways, in clubs, assemblies, above all in the press and in journals, or perhaps only in unspoken feelings of each one of us (4); of the common man in the street or of a small circle of the cultured (8); here a true power factor, which statesmen must take into account, or something of no political significance (5); something again to be evaluated differently in every country (5 or 6); sometimes united, rising up like a tidal wave against the government and the experts, sometimes divided, concealing conflicting tendencies (7); at one time bringing out the simple and natural sentiments of the people, at another time being the rowdy thoughtless manifestations of wild instincts (6); always leading and always being led (5, 3); looked down upon by the sophisticated, yet forcing the hands of men (6, 5); contagious like an epidemic (10); capricious, treacherous (9); and power mad (resembling man himself) (6); and then again only a word by which those in power are bewitched (5).[2]

Now, what is interesting about this bewildering formulation is that it can be disentangled easily as soon as one matches it against what one might call *a complete attitude distribution.* Oncken undoubtedly gives a definition of public opinion. It is a statistical distribution of utterances (1 and 7) expressed by various segments of the population (2), and these segments can and should be classified by the degree of their competence (8). But intermingled with this definition are a number of empirical problems which are encountered in investigations more complicated than cross-national surveys. What factors determine a given attitude distribution at any given time (3)? What effect does it have on statesmen and on the legislative process in general (5)? How are opinions communicated and diffused (10)?

Three further elements in this passage foreshadow contemporary concerns. How should one choose among the various sources and devices which can be used to ascertain an attitude distribution (4)? Oncken mentions only expressions at meetings and in the printed mass media. Today we would, of course, add questionnaires and other more systematic research procedures. And we would now translate the phrase "capricious, treacherous" (9) into the terminology of panel techniques, distinguishing people who in repeated interviews show constant attitudes from those whose attitudes fluctuate. Finally (6), Oncken is obviously concerned with the normative problem of how certain opinions should be evaluated.

It seemed worthwhile to give a concrete example of the possible relation between the humanistic tradition and the world of today's social research, where we classify people according to their personal characteristics, the content and the intensity of the attitudes they have, and their level of information. The creation of adequate instruments of classification is usually called measurement; I shall use this term in a very broad sense, without entering into any of the usual discussions as to the differences between measurement in the natural and the social sciences.

Measurement. Most of the books dealing with attitudes now have appendices, explaining how various specific questions and other indicators were combined into more complex indices. Thus, for instance, *The People's Choice* reports indices of political interest; Valdimer Orlando Key classifies people according to the strength of their attachment to various organizations; Hadley Cantril and Lloyd A. Free distinguish between ideological and operational liberalism.[3] The techniques used in all these studies are too well known to need further elaboration. In general, it is not possible to reconstruct such measures from the past. However, strangely enough, one of the more complex approaches is applicable to historical material. I have in mind the so-called projective tests.

The psychologist David McClelland has developed a test to find out how ambitious a person is.[4] He has constructed a number of vaguely designed pictures wherein a group of people talk to each other, a man sits at his desk at night, or a father walks with his young son along a road.

Subjects to whom the pictures are shown are asked to invent an appropriate story. Does the group swap jokes, or do they plan to build something in their village? Does the man at the desk read a detective story, or work? Does the father admonish the son to improve his scholastic standing? People are scored according to how much planning, ambition, need for achievement, they impute to the characters in the pictures. This supposedly permits one to measure what, in another context, might be called entrepreneurial spirit. As a matter of fact, McClelland has used his test in a number of underdeveloped countries to make a guess as to how soon one can expect the much-discussed economic "take-off." In these places such material collected today should be useful to a historian who, thirty years hence, tries to explain what happened in the meantime.

This technique can be applied to documentary materials of all kinds. A typical example is a study by Norman M. Bradburn and David E. Berlew.[5] They wanted to show that this need for achievement is historically related to economic activities. For the period between 1400 and 1850 they sampled three kinds of English literature: dramas, reports on sea voyages, and street ballads. As an economic index they used available data on the importation of coal through the harbor of London. They classified their material into periods of fifty years. A graph makes it reasonably convincing that changes in the index of economic productivity were always preceded, in an interval of about two generations, by changes in the emphasis on achievement in English literature. A number of similar studies have used the cross-cultural files at Yale, relating, for instance, the content of tribal legends with prevailing child-rearing practices. Obviously, one has to wait for many more studies of this kind before the method can be trusted as a tool of historical research. But these early efforts certainly deserve attention.

Perhaps some of you have doubts about the validity of such a procedure. Then, let me tell you that one great historian has used it, at least for the sake of argumentation. In 1827 Thomas Babington Macaulay wanted to explain why Machiavelli was so misunderstood by French and German readers. His argument runs about as follows. At the end of the Middle Ages the Italian cities had developed a middle-class culture of artisans and merchants, while the countries north of the Alps were still in a barbarous state. In the north, courage was the main means of survival: courage to withstand the hardships of life, and courage to repel hostile hordes which were incessantly threatening each other with war. In the Italian cities, ingenuity was the most cherished ability: ingenuity in improving the protective value of the community, and ingenuity in meeting the competition of fellow citizens in an essentially democratic society. "Hence, while courage was a point of honor in other countries, ingenuity became the point of honor in Italy."

Macaulay struggles hard to make his point clear and convincing to his reader. First of all he compares an English and an Italian hero. Henry V was admired by the English, in spite of his personal crudeness and cruelty, because he won a great battle. Francesco Sforza was admired by the Italians, in spite of his personal treachery and faithlessness, because he was a successful statesman. And still, Macaulay is not yet quite sure that the reader has seen the matter clearly. He finally hits upon what seems to him a useful literary device:

> We have illustrated our meaning by an instance taken from history. We will select another from fiction. Othello murders his wife; he gives orders for the murder of his lieutenant; he ends by murdering himself. *Yet he never loses the esteem and affection of Northern readers.* His intrepid and ardent spirit redeems everything. The unsuspecting confidence with which he listens to his advisor, the agony with which he shrinks from the thought of shame, the tempest of passion with which he commits his crimes, and the haughty fearlessness with which he avows them, give an extraordinary interest to his character. Iago, on the contrary, is the object of universal loathing. . . . *Now we suspect that an Italian audience in the fifteenth century would have felt very differently.* Othello would have inspired nothing but detestation and contempt. The folly with which he trusts the friendly professions of a man whose promotion he had obstructed, the credulity with which he takes unsupported assertions, and trivial circumstances, for unanswerable proofs, the violence with which he silences the exculpation till the exculpation can only aggravate his misery, would have excited the abhorrence and disgust of the spectators. The conduct of Iago they would assuredly have condemned; but they would have condemned it as we condemn that of his victim. Something of interest and respect would have mingled with their disapprobation. The readiness of the traitor's wit, the clearness of his judgment, the skill with which he penetrates the dispositions of others and conceals his own, would have ensured to him a certain portion of their esteem.[6]

It is clear what Macaulay is striving for. He wishes someone had conducted attitude studies in fifteenth century Florence and London. The

Othello story could have been written up in one or two paragraphs, without giving either Othello or Iago any advantage. Pretests could have been conducted to make sure the wording was quite unbiased. (Perhaps they might have concealed the fact that Othello was black because that might bias some respondents.) The crucial question would have been: How many Florentines and Londoners, respectively, approve of Iago, how many of Othello, and how many say "don't know"?

In a way, measurements, scales, variables (I shall use the terms interchangeably) provide the basic vocabulary for the language of social research. To form meaningful propositions, they have to be related to each other. This is done by cross-tabulation or, as it is generally called now, multivariate analysis.

Multivariate Analysis. We usually start with one piece of information in which we are especially interested: an attitude toward a specific issue, a vote, intention, etc.; usually this item is called the criterion, or the dependent variable. We then begin to make further distinctions. Is the dependent variable distributed differently in various social groups, or in different regions? Are people in different organizations characterized by different attitude distributions—for instance, are professors in private universities more "progressive" than those in state universities? There is, obviously, no limit to the kind of distinctions we can explore. The situation is somewhat similar to what a chemist does when he investigates a new substance. In what kind of liquid does it dissolve, if at all? What happens if we heat it or try to deform it with instruments of various strengths? Using whatever other tools he has available, the chemist will become ever better acquainted with the nature of the substance.

Moving away from this analogy, one can list a few of the uses the survey analyst makes of his multivariate analysis. He finds that older people read fewer books. Does it mean that old age extinguishes interest? In a cross-sectional sample taken today in the United States, one will always find that older people are less-educated. By cross-tabulating reading habits simultaneously against age and education, we find that age plays only a small role; in each age group, the less-educated read less. The older working women are, the greater is their rate of absenteeism. But, the older women are more likely to be married and have more family duties. The survey analyst, by proper cross-tabulation, can establish the relative weight of physiological age and family status. Sometimes a multivariate analysis permits us to refine an initial finding. It is well known that in the United States at large, women go to the polls less frequently than men. But, if we introduce as a further variable socio-economic status, we find that this difference is very small in privileged strata, while it is very large in underprivileged strata. This is a lead to investigate further how the family structure, especially among new immigrants, affects the civic role of women.

A special variation on the theme of multivariate analysis is provided by the comparison of two surveys, or two related questions in the same survey. Political scientists of the nineteenth century sometimes suspected that it was not only public opinion which affects the work of the legislator. Sometimes the flow seemed to go in the opposite direction. Several cases are now documented where the enactment of a law changed public opinion in the direction of approving its content. The second type of comparison is exemplified by an especially perspicacious analysis in a recent study of the British election of 1964.[7] Prospective voters were given a list of qualities by which candidates could be described. Two questions were asked: Which of these qualities is most important for running the country later? Which of them is most likely to be revealed on television?

I selected three groups of qualities, each represented by two examples. The first group refers to occupational characteristics: hard-working, able. Among 800 respondents, this quality is mentioned 400 times as important, but only 150 times as being visible on television; undoubtedly, a reasonable finding. Personal qualities—kind, unassuming—are mentioned 40 times as important, but 80 times as visible on television; this, again, makes all-round sense. But, then there is a group of two qualities which one might call moral: sincere and straightforward. They are mentioned 500 times as important, which shows the concern people have with the honesty of public figures. But 650 answers consider that this kind of morality can be judged by watching a candidate on television. Anyone familiar with the way television can be used to manufacture a candidate will be rather worried by the fact that the general public is not aware of this possibility.

A major area of convergence between multivariate analysis and historiography comes from elections studies. The man who has systematically charted this field is Lee Benson. I am sure all of you know his programmatic statement.[8] The basic idea is that one cannot understand the outcome of a specific election without making comparisons in space and time. What he calls "space" corresponds to what was just described as subgroups. Jackson's popular plurality in 1824 was due to an overwhelming majority in only a few states. Lincoln's victory in 1860 could not be credited to a special German-American vote, because in most states the voters of German descent followed the regional proportions. Consideration for long-term time trends are, of course, especially important for historians. The Republican defeat in 1884 could not have been due to the personal turpitude of Blaine, because it was part of a decline in the Republican vote, which was already highly visible in the 1882 congressional election. Bryan might have wanted to appeal to the urban proletariat, but a detailed analysis of the 1896 election returns shows that this appeal was not successful. In a subsequent study Benson made skillful use of multivariate analysis to show that ethnic, rather than socio-economic differences, seemed to have greater weight.[9] In the study of coat-tail effects, one compares the vote for President to the vote for senators and congressmen.

Benson's research strategy could be used as a textbook to exemplify all the points made so far. He first takes rather vague statements on election outcomes, as they are found in history texts, and reformulates them so that they can be tested by the election data themselves. Then he subdivides the population so that the differential voting record of small areas can be used for the purpose of interpretation. Once he knows specifically who voted for whom, he can take known characteristics of these subgroups to make plausible inferences of what attracted them toward a specific candidate. Obviously, for this final step he has to draw on all the documentary material that historians traditionally use. As a political-sociologist, I have to say that this combination of narrative and detailed statistics makes fascinating reading.

Just for the record, it should be added that even this material cannot be completely free from what is often called the ecological fallacy. Only since the existence of public opinion polls is it possible to classify voters by their individual characteristics. There will always be districts where, say, Poles and Jews are equally represented and it might, therefore, not be possible to attribute the district to one specific ethnic group. But, by using a small enough unit and by careful management of aggregated evidence, this whole approach has undoubtedly added much to the understanding of the political past. On this point a suggestion for future research might be permitted. Regional and local polls are becoming increasingly available.[10] It would be an interesting experiment to carry out two types of analysis separately, one based on the voting records of small districts, the other based on the analysis of individual voters. Would a comparison of the findings show close agreement? Would not extended analysis of these agreements contribute to further understanding?

Beyond Surveys. The dominant role of surveys, which started in the early 1930s, was deplored by some sociologists. They objected to the fact that surveys atomize the social world, while the main task of the sociologist should be to take into account larger social entities and the way they influence the behavior of the people involved in them. There have been essentially four different ways in which this justified objection has been met. Two of them might not be of particular interest to historians, and I will mention them only briefly. Two others deserve more careful attention.

One device was to develop variations on the traditional sampling procedures. Thus, for instance, James S. Coleman describes the idea of snowball sampling.

> One method of interviewing a man's immediate social environment is to use the sociometric questions in the interview for sampling purposes. For example, in a study of political attitudes in a New England community, Martin Trow has used this approach: first interviewing a small sample of persons, then asking these persons who their best friends are, interviewing these friends, then asking *them* their friends, interviewing these, and so on. In this way, the sampling plan follows out the chains of sociometric relations in the community. In many respects, this sampling technique is like that of a good reporter who tracks down "leads" from one person to another. The difference, of course, is that snowball sampling in survey research is amenable to the same scientific sampling procedures as ordinary samples. Where the population in ordinary samples is a population of individuals, here it is two populations: one of individuals and one of *relations* among individuals.[11]

Another development was what Peter Blau called the study of structural effects.[12] It also begins with a new type of sampling, but moves from there in a different direction. An example would be a study of the effect of McCarthyism on American social science professors. First, a sample of colleges was chosen; then, within each college, the teachers were sampled. The reaction of the teachers to the events of these difficult years turned out to be quite different in elite colleges and in more conventional institutions, in state as compared to private universities, etc. The role of the context has been shown in many other studies. The vocational choices of students depend not only upon the social status of their parents, but also upon the social composition of the schools they attend. The self-esteem of young people is related not to their religion, but whether their religion is dominant or deviant in the neighborhood in which they live. The vote of various occupational groups is affected by the social composition of the total community.

Historians are, of course, used to taking regional differences into account. But methodological attention to such contextual propositions might open up new avenues of investigation. The example most closely joining the two fields comes from Seymour M. Lipset.[13] He compared the vote in the 1860 election with the referendum on secession in the Southern states a few months later. The units of his analysis were counties. The South, during the election, was divided between two factions of the Democratic Party, with Douglas representing the moderate, and Brecken-ridge representing the radical wing. One would have expected that in the referendum the politically moderate counties would vote against secession, while the Breckenridge counties would vote for it. For the South at large there was, however, very little relation between the two votes. And when the counties were divided according to the extent of their slaveholdings, an even more surprising fact turned up. The counties with large slave-holdings had predominantly voted the moderate wing, but were for secession a short time later. For the counties with small slaveholdings, the opposite relation held true. Lipset's interpretation was that the vote during the election was still guided by sectional party tradition, without much attention to the content of the campaign; at the time of the referendum on secession, economic interest prevailed. Historians will want to study Lipset's substantive story in detail. My purpose is to draw your attention to the methodological idea.

I now turn to the two other directions in which social research moved to meet the "holistic challenge."

Organizational Research. Larger social units can provide the contexts in which individual conduct may be studied. But these collectives can themselves become the objectives of social research. In recent years, partly due to the availability of larger funds, systematic studies of organizations have been carried out. Factories, hospitals, schools were characterized according to major dimensions, similar to the way in which personalities previously had been studied. The size of organizations, the span of command, the diversity of personnel, the complexity of subdivisions are examples of such organizational characteristics.[14] The topics investigated can be divided conventionally into two large groups. The static studies inquire into the relation between organizational variables: which types of organization are more efficient, what is the balance of satisfaction between different segments, etc? The dynamic studies are mainly concerned with the way organizational change comes about.

Studies of organizational change can in turn be divided once more. There are those where the change comes about by the "dialectic" of the organization's work itself. A famous example is Philip Selznik's study of the Tennessee Valley Authority.[15] The authority's main goal was to help the small farmer; but it was also supposed to mobilize regional support. The public relations sector of TVA felt that local support had to be gained by engaging the support of local leadership, which was in the hands of large farmers. In pursuing its "sub-goal," the public relations people slowly forced a change in the general policy of TVA, away from its primary concern with the small farmers of the region. The other type of change study is more concerned with the role of external factors. These could be technological elements, like the effect of introducing large computers on the internal power structure of a company, or they could be environmental elements; for instance, what happens when a company moves away from the center of the city to a suburban region.

For both types of change study, I can give a historical example, one explicitly, and the other more tacitly influenced by sociological considerations. An intrinsically generated change is investigated in Sigmund Diamond's study of the earlier stages of the Virginia Colony.[16] According to this author, the colony began as a chartered business organization, but soon suffered from a scarcity of labor. To get Europeans to come overseas, considerable concessions had to be made in terms of property, as well as civil rights. This in turn changed the relation between the labor force and management to the point where, using Diamond's expression, an organization was converted into a society.

An example of extrinsic change is provided by Bernard Bailyn's monograph on the origins of American politics.[17] He wants to analyze what happened to English political institutions when they were transplanted to the American environment. He first describes the situation in England in the early part of the eighteenth century. According to the formal Constitution, the balance of power between Crown and Parliament much favored the latter, but the Crown had many informal ways to hold its own. The franchise was restricted by property requirements; rotten boroughs were easily manipulated; many sinecures were available to tempt members of Parliament. But the formal Constitution did not permit the same informal correctives when transferred to the colonies. A much larger number of people owned the small plot of land needed to assure the voting rights, there were no rotten boroughs, and the governors had very few jobs to give away. This kind of "organizational change" is the pivotal idea around which Bailyn explains the beginning of the American Revolution.

Many other topics in the theory of organization would find their analogies in the historian's workshop: problems of succession—what happens when the same role is filled by a sequence of different persons; organizational intelligence—the adequate collection and use of information. But, the most concrete and visible convergence between history and sociology has come about in the recent efforts of sociologists to deal more globally with larger social units.

Macrosociology. This is the name under which the movement has come to be known; its origin is easily traced. The temporary dominance of survey studies created uneasiness among younger American sociologists: for various reasons the profession did not deal with broad social issues; at international congresses these men came in contact with European colleagues who pointed out that American sociology had lost its contact with the humanistic tradition; and most of all, the concern of the United States with underdeveloped countries shifted attention to the sociological aspects of the political scene.

Not surprisingly, then, examples of recent macrosociological studies deal with major political problems. Ralf Dahrendorf wants to know why

Germany did not develop a stable democracy, while Harry Eckstein analyzes factors leading to the opposite situation in Norway.[18] The role of the citizen under various political conditions is investigated: Inkeles and Bauer do so for Russia, and Marshall for England; Etzioni and Eisenstadt raise, each in his own way, the question of unification.[19] How are smaller territorial and political units successfully combined into larger formations, and when do such efforts fail? It is not the topics, however, that are important for the present discussion, but the methods used. In which ways are they different from the historian's approach?

A superficial answer is easily given. The historian does his best to trace a case in all its details. The sociologist always has some generalization in mind. But what are the prerequisites of such generalizations? Two different trends can be distinguished. One might be called statistical.

Modern sociology started as an effort to understand what happened to society as a result of industrialization. It was macrosociology to begin with, but without any methodological self-consciousness. Then came, first slowly and later with increasing speed, the concern with evidence, which culminated in the survey movement I characterized above. Now that the interest in large-scale topics has been revived, it is not possible to forget the variable-language so characteristic of modern social research. Therefore, this language was transferred, but on a higher level than previously. Partly this happened in a very explicit way. I am sure you are all aware of the interest in international data banks. All statistical information available for a country is put on IBM cards, and studies are based on cross-tabulations of these data. A recently published book, entitled *Comparing Nations,* is characteristic of this tendency.[20] What happened there is that the language of social research, which had already been elevated from individuals to organizations, was now further raised to the national level.

But this is not what I want to discuss. The more interesting development in the present context is the way in which writers dealt only with one or a few cases and carried out their analysis *as if* they had such variables available. If you have ever looked at a textbook in introductory sociology, you will have noted that it tries mainly to bring order into the bewildering complexity of social experience. The terminologies are not fixed, but you will almost always find distinctions between different sectors of society, such as the economic, political, and cultural. Then come institutions: the family, the school, the church. Cross-cutting are associations, such as unions, political parties, clubs. And finally, social relations between people as well as groups are characterized by "prevailing norms," of which Parsons' pattern variables are a distinctive example. Whatever else a sociologist does, he is trained to reduce the world to a small number of concepts, units, dimensions—whatever these subdivisions might be called. The macrosociologists draw upon this reservoir and come up with what we might call macrovariables. Lipset, in tracing the origins of the United States, centers around two such concepts: the early Americans' equality and their achievement.[21] Half of Lipset's book is a variation on the theme of how these two values played on each other to explain the emergence of new institutions. Equality can deteriorate into populism, which is restrained by the achievement motive. The latter can deteriorate into rapacious acquisitiveness, which is kept in line by legislation growing out of equality concepts. The two together make for conformity which is more profitable than rebellion in a system of rapid social mobility.

Another distinction frequent in macrosociological literature is that between a public and a private sphere of life. In trying to make contemporary Burma understandable, Lucian W. Pye takes as a centerpiece of its whole history the fact that the Burmese never distinguished between the two spheres.[22] Dahrendorf finds it characteristic of Germany that the private sphere has dominance over the public, while in Anglo-Saxon countries the opposite is true.

Sometimes one major sociological variable is made to carry the whole story. Walter G. Runciman takes from Stouffer's *American Soldier* the notion of relative deprivation.[23] People judge their own social position not in absolute terms, but relative to other groups with which they compare themselves. The reference groups can either be close to their own status or socially more distant. Runciman later tries to explain the history of the British labor movement since World War I by the fact that British workers never really compared themselves with the middle classes in their country. It is not possible in a limited space to develop these ideas in more detail, but those of you who follow up some of this literature will notice how a rather small number of macrosociological variables reappear from study to study. Parsimony is cherished, while the historian is likely to take pride in the richness of detail. A comparable difference can be noticed when interpretations are called for.

I am sure all of you know the extensive literature on the logic of explanation in history. Writers usually line up on either side of an argument which Carl Gustav Hempel started. According to him, every explanation proceeds in the following steps. There is a general law connecting a number of variables and containing several free parameters. A specific event is characterized by specific values of these parameters. The combination of the "covering law" and the specific parameters provides the explanation. The chief opponent of this view is William H. Dray, who feels that only a full narrative giving weight to unique events is acceptable as an explanatory account.[24]

Hempel himself has suggested a possible compromise by introducing the notion of "explanation sketches." These are schemata in which the covering law is not really known, the parameters of the concrete situation are vague, and in which, therefore, any concrete explanation is more or less distant from a rigorous analysis. I am sure that few sociologists are aware of this debate, but they have been conditioned to use a small number of explanation sketches for a variety of reasons. One major source of this habit of thought is the notion of social systems. The idea is that society consists of component parts, which must maintain a sort of equilibrium if the whole system is to remain viable. A change in one part induces necessary changes in other parts, until a new equilibrium is achieved. A typical explanation sketch, then, consists in tracing this re-equilibration.

As an example, take Marshall's discussion of the development of citizenship in England. According to him, citizenship has three components: civil rights, political rights, and social rights—incidentally, another example of variable language writ large. In the small medieval community those three elements are taken care of as long as the dominance of the feudal lord is accepted. After a while the man in the street and the man in the field request further civil rights, which are guaranteed by courts that cut across feudal prerogatives. But now these courts, as national institutions, are located at a far distance from the individual communities, and appointed at an even more distant center. Therefore, the control of those new legal institutions becomes urgent, and the battle for political rights necessarily follows.

An example from another sphere is Neil J. Smelser's detailed analysis of factory legislation in the early phases of the British cotton industry.[25] In the middle of the eighteenth century the British family of the lower classes was a small, integrated system which performed a great diversity of functions, including weaving. With the beginning of manufacturing, the whole family was transferred to the mills. To an outsider, Smelser makes a convincing case that the early factory workers wanted to maintain the family as a functional unit; for example, they rejected shorter hours for children, because parents would not have known where their children were when not working. Only after the idea developed that the family's various functions could be separated from each other was it possible for the nineteenth century factory legislation to develop. Instead, then, of emphasizing a growth in philanthropic sentiment, Smelser describes the period, say from 1800 to 1840, as a slow mutual readjustment of different parts of the broader social system.

The explanation of changes, in terms of a system's schema, goes under the name of functional analysis in our trade. Another type of sketch has a very different source. Some sociologists have made detailed studies of what might be called mass decisions. Some of these decisions are institutionally prescribed. By election day everyone has to decide for whom he will vote, if at all. In addition to analyzing election returns, one can obviously interview people as to how they made up their minds; as a matter of fact, in a more up-to-date design, they are interviewed several times during the campaign to watch, so to say, the votes in the making.[26] Other decisions are also made collectively, but are not so strictly timed. There are statistical studies showing that migration from one country to another is roughly correlated with the economic situation of both the country of origin and the target of the move. But, within this broad frame, it is still very important to know the evolution of these decisions: how did people learn of the target country, what specific incidents crystallized the move, etc. Other decisions are even more dispersed. Some sociologists, I among them, do not shy away from studying why housewives buy a certain brand of coffee or why men shift from one brand of cigars to another.

The techniques of this empirical analysis of decisions have been developed to quite a refined state. It is of no avail just to ask people why they did a certain thing. If one wants to get information that is comparable and accessible to statistical treatment, one must use *accounting schemes,* the elements of which have to be provided in every interview. A Puerto Rican who migrated to New York may say he did so on the advice of a relative already there; here, the channel of influence is established right away. But what, in turn, did the relative stress: higher wages, more freedom, the attractions of the big city?[27] Inversely, if someone moves to the Southwest hoping that the dry air will cure his asthma, how did he learn about it: the rough advice of a doctor, publicity of the local chamber of commerce, an acquaintance who had gone there before? The distinction between the channels of influence and the substantive nature of attractive features is only one of the many that must be made in such accounting schemes. The social norms which facilitate or delay a decision have to be established, even if individual respondents are only dimly aware of them; the time it takes to arrive at a decision and the characteristic phases through which it moves must all be taken into account. (This last aspect has found special attention in studies of the acceptance of innovations among farmers.)[28]

The specific character of these accounting schemes will often differ from one topic to the next, but their role is always the same. They provide an abstract schema of the decision studied.[29] It forces the investigator to fill in, in case after case, the concrete facts required in each part of the schema, and it brings out in great clarity the need to assess the relative weight of the various parts of the schema. While the studies I referred to may seem trivial at first glance, it is obvious that the historian meets the same problem on a variety of levels: when he deals with a decision of a major political personality, when he wants to explain the participation of whole groups of people in social movements, or when he personalizes a whole country as one decision maker. The accounting scheme then becomes another case of an explanation sketch. Only certain aspects of the whole event are singled out for analysis. Occasionally, historians have made the connection. Thus, Ernest R. May's study on opinion leadership during the Spanish-American War starts explicitly from empirical decision studies made by sociologists.[30] I venture that many discussions among historians on "the causes of" or "the reasons why" would profit from attention to this technique.

You may feel that I have digressed from the topic of macrosociology. But I really have not. I claimed that macrosociologists use only a rather small number of explanation sketches. This is because their imagery is taken from a limited number of sociological traditions. I gave two examples: the general ideas of functional analysis and the specific procedures of empirical decision studies. Fortunately, limitations of space and time do not permit the inclusion of other ones; I would have trouble finding more examples in which the basic ideas have been explicated in enough detail.

My emphasis so far has been on the actual and potential role of methods of sociological research in the work of historians. This is partly because it is the side of the question with which I am most familiar, and partly because I think that this is, indeed, the way in which social disciplines influence each other most. Still, there are a number of substantive sociological ideas which historians have found useful.

Other Connections. Richard Hofstadter has given a personal account of how he saw "new problems which a historian has usually ignored."[31] He provides quite a number of examples: social status and mobility, generational conflicts, mass culture, etc. Other examples come easily to mind. The intense interest of sociologists in social stratification has certainly introduced into historical writings the notion of elites or opinion leaders, and has made them more sensitive to differentiations between various social groups.

In addition, a number of sociological concerns have given rise to new problems then taken up by historians or pursued further by sociologists. Public opinion itself has emerged as a topic of historical research. Much of the primary material comes from France. Even before the Revolution, the regional intendants were expected to provide the Paris court with periodic reports on social conditions and sentiments in their administrative areas. Bernard Lecuyer, in a forthcoming book, has unearthed most surprising examples. Thus, for instance, in the middle of the eighteenth century the intendants were supposed to start rumors about intended tax legislation: the king's ministers wanted to know which of the proposals would meet with resistance. The reports of the intendants were based on reports they in turn requested from local police and judicial officers. This base material is still preserved in some of the regional archives. One day it will make a fascinating study to see what the intendants selected when they wrote their own reports. (This is a historical version of contemporary inquiries that analyze what selections a newspaper makes from the news services it subscribes to.) In another study it was possible to follow the course of these regional reports upwards into the deliberations of the French cabinet. Lynn M. Case analyzed the minutes of meetings held under the chairmanship of Napoleon III.[32] In 1866, at the beginning of the Prussian-Austrian War, it was in the interest of the Second Empire to support the Austrians, in order to forestall the expansion of Prussia. But the regional reports available to the cabinet showed that a war-like movement could easily lead to popular upheavals, and so the emperor decided on neutrality.

The study of mass communications has also had its impact on historical scholarship. I do not need to mention content analysis, which has been used so aptly by other participants in this symposium. But mass media have not only been studied; they have been hotly debated among sociologists. Some of the more philosophical minded are sure that television poses a great cultural threat; the empiricists cannot find much evidence at the moment, and wonder whether the whole problem is not badly formulated.[33] Leo Lowenthal was able to show that any time a new form of cultural distribution developed, some critics felt it had dangerous cultural consequences: it was feared that lending libraries and popular magazines would lower the level of literary creation.[34] Perhaps they did; but in the symposium just mentioned I reminded the participants how Plato was sure the invention of writing weakened man's memory, and thereby his creativity.

One can suggest further topics of historical research. Today, as members of the lonely crowd in a mass society, we can read a new publication every month telling us about the spirit of our times. When did this collective self-consciousness start? I have found and previously reported occasional references that Goethe was concerned with "the general trend of the contemporary world toward an average civilization," and Carlyle complained that it had become difficult to do "a piece of spiritual work" because, instead, one had to "call a public meeting, appoint committees, issue prospectuses" (today we would say write project proposals). But after all, that was the time when many other writers began to discuss social change. Were the men of the Renaissance, two hundred years earlier, aware that they had now become individualists, or did they have to wait for Burckhardt to tell them so in retrospect?

Another topic of contemporary history would be to explore more fully the actual institutional arrangements between historians and sociologists, as they have emerged since the beginning of this century. When the German Sociological Society was created in 1910, its first secretary, Max

Weber, proposed a study of the German newspaper system, which was supposed to be a combined historical and sociological inquiry.[35] Nothing came of it. The first successful and seminal creation of which I know occurred after World War I: the French *Annales,* of which Marc Bloch was a founder and the most famous exponent. After World War II the Social Science Research Council published relevant bulletins, and somewhat later in England, as well as in this country, journals devoted to the borderline areas between the two fields appeared. An analysis of the conditions under which these efforts came about and the sociometry of the participants should be undertaken before the source material is lost. Finally, I might be permitted to repeat a suggestion I first made almost twenty years ago. The major polling agencies often ask questions of a general nature, just to satisfy the contract requirements of their newspaper clients. Why do we not create a joint commission of historians and polling agencies to formulate questions from time to time that are likely to be of interest to future historians?[36]

It is only fair to end my remarks on a note of reverse lend-lease. No one can deny that we sociologists owe many debts to historians. At least three of them should be singled out. For one, we are always in danger of omitting the historical dimension of our own work. I once did a study of an upstate New York county and explained my findings in the light of the clear conservative character of the area. Later, I was made aware that fifty years ago it was a center of the beginning Socialist movement. Lloyd Warner, after *Yankee City* appeared, was told that for a long time the town had not been nearly as Yankee as he assumed. It gives one pause to imagine what difference this knowledge would have made, although so far as I know, neither one of us has yet had time for this pause.

Of more immediate impact could be certain skills of historians. Community studies and other forms of participant observation are still important parts of sociological activities; as a matter of fact, recently they have regained some of their former prominence. Much of this work requires picking up observational cues, interpreting them imaginatively, and then searching for cumulative evidence. One way I train my students is to carefully read with them certain historical writings, such as Huizinga's chapter on the violent temper of the waning Middle Ages. He first reconstructs the environment: the continuous ringing of bells, the stench in the streets. Then he collects evidence on the temper itself: duels resulting from chess games, the delight in public executions. Finally, he traces consequences: efforts to repress this violence by complicated rituals, by obsessive classifications which attach names to all kinds of objects. Such a work, together with some of the anthropological classics, is an important step in developing aptitudes for field work.

Most of all, the historian is indispensable for the macrosociologists. Several of their major spokesmen have stressed that they can seldom go back to primary sources; they have to start with the data historians have collected and interpreted. A few years ago UNESCO initiated a broad survey on contemporary trends in the "Sciences Sociales et Humaines." There are two main sections, one dealing with nomothetic disciplines, the other with idiographic disciplines. The historians are in the latter division and I represent sociology in the former. In this capacity I am making a detailed analysis of about twenty major studies which straddle the border-line of our two disciplines. I hope that some of you will ask me for my reading list and check my homework. I am convinced that interdisci-plinary relations—and that is what I am talking about today—cannot be clarified by the discussion of principles but only by careful scrutiny of ongoing effects.

Comment 2

◆

Bradford Perkins

DEPARTMENT OF HISTORY, UNIVERSITY OF MICHIGAN

MOST HISTORIANS would admit that their profession is, in general, conservative and cautious. Most would agree that the discipline still has much to learn from the social sciences, including sociology. Lazarsfeld has pointed to some of the methodologies and techniques historians might well employ to give added dimensions to their own work, and there is no doubt that these approaches can give fruitful results. Indeed, some of them have already done so; for example, Merle Curti's study of Trempealeau County or Lee Benson's assessment of Jacksonianism in New York State. Yet, for various reasons most of the sociological approaches also have their dangers for the historian. These dangers are so serious that it seems probable that, on the whole, sociology will communicate insights and suggest strategies to the historian more often than it will provide him with unchallengeable answers to vexing questions. The studies of Sigmund Diamond and of Bernard Bailyn, mentioned by Lazarsfeld as examples of the organizational approach applied to history, fall into the former category. Neither, it seems to me, displaces (or even claims to displace) earlier interpretations of the same questions by employing a different technique, but each study sharpens our understanding by employing, particularly in Diamond's case, insights, language, descriptive terminology, and categorization borrowed from the sociologist.

Lazarsfeld's paper exposes two of the dangers that face the historian when he looks to sociology for help. The first of these is very simply the difficulty and in very many cases the impossibility of gathering data of sufficient quantity and quality to support confident generalizations. This problem is clearly revealed by several of the works on American history cited by Lazarsfeld. The very valuable and provocative study by Lee Benson has, along with the quite different work of John William Ward and Marvin Meyers, transformed our views of the Jacksonian period.[37] Benson deals with a problem little more than a century removed from our own time. Yet, for his exercise in multivariate analysis, he could not freely choose between the various elections of the Jacksonian period; he was the prisoner of the decennial census and therefore, as critics like Frank O. Gattell have argued,[38] may have failed to examine the potentially most revealing canvass of that period. (It might be added, as Benson himself points out, that we still do not know if the New York pattern is repeated in other states.) Moving on in time, we come to Seymour M. Lipset's brief survey of the election of 1860 and the Southern secession movement. Lipset generalized on the basis of published materials available to him in the 1950s. A few years later, after arduous work in a mass of previously unused material, Ralph A. Wooster produced a study which directly controverted several of Lipset's conclusions and sharply modified others.[39] The result was a far less clear and consistent picture than Lipset had supposed. Finally, to comment upon another example cited by Lazarsfeld, Ernest May's recent study of American imperialism at the end of the nineteenth century, and in particular of the attitude of the American elite toward that imperialism, shows the problem the historian faces. May has read deeply in the sociological literature, and his monograph rests upon his understanding of that literature. But, even for the years just before 1900, adequate data appears simply to be unavailable. For May's purposes the composition of the American elite is critically important, and yet he is unable to determine it in a convincing fashion, being forced, for example, to depend upon a single fugitive reference to an individual in the *Chicago Tribune* as a guide. The "information explosion" of our own time may make it possible for future historians to speak with confidence about problems analogous to those treated by Benson and May. For the moment, both authors and readers must exercise caution.

Lazarsfeld's paper quite correctly points out a major difference between the sociological approach—or at least an important contemporary emphasis in sociology—and the approach employed by most historians today. As he says, in sociology "parsimony is cherished, while the historian is likely to take pride in the richness of detail." At another point he comments, "the historian does his best to trace a case in all its details. The sociologist always has some generalization in mind." This indictment of historians—for such I take it to be—has much force. We are all only too well aware—and we are constantly reminded by reviews in scholarly journals as well as by the books which come before us—that historians often become mired in detail, that they produce not only sheer description but often meaningless description of events and developments which have only a very narrow interest and meaning. But there are dangers in overconfident generalization as well. There is also the risk that generalization, particularly if it precedes the gathering of evidence, will oversimplify the historical process, that it will distort and flatten our picture of the incredibly variegated topography that most historical problems present. The historian has the duty to generalize, to emphasize cause and connection, but he also has the duty to suggest the infinite variety provided by the interplay of large numbers of men and influences. To take but two examples, again from American history but not cited by Lazarsfeld, it seems to me that the Marxist approach employed by Eugene J. Genovese in his study, the most valuable recent contribution to our understanding of the slave system, and the economic determinism of William A. Williams, a prolific and stimulating student of modern American diplomacy, are sources of weakness as well as strength.[40] In the work of both, the emphasis is fresh and important, but an unwillingness to recognize the complexity of the historical process has caused the two authors to carry generalization too far.

It is possible, then, for historians to become bemused by techniques successfully employed for different purposes in other disciplines. History can, and must, continue to search more broadly in those disciplines for suggestive approaches, for insights, perhaps even for methodology in the precise sense of that term. At the same time, the historian cannot allow himself to conclude that his present approaches and above all his present skepticism are worthless. The nature of historical evidence is, and for most problems will remain, very different from that of the evidence employed by most sociologists. The nature of historical explanation is, and for most problems will remain, far more complex than that employed by some sociologists dealing with different issues in a quite different way. In the search for generalizations, or what Lazarsfeld calls "parsimony," the historian can easily go astray. He should, I think, exercise caution, and he should remain a skeptic, always knowing that it is unlikely that there is some easy road to absolute historical truth.

3

As we have seen, historians long have been fascinated with the study of public opinion. Although a historical analysis of opinion or image is interesting, it obviously becomes more meaningful when it can be demonstrated that the opinion had an effect on policy. Unfortunately, historians have been generally unsuccessful and unconvincing in their attempts to link causally opinion to policy. Most facilely accept the rhetoric of politician-statesmen who report that their policies have always responded to or reflected public opinion. Significantly, the most popular diplomatic history text book is entitled A Diplomatic History of the American People.

Bernard C. Cohen, a political scientist, has examined this problem in The Political Process and Foreign Policy (1957) *and* The Press and Foreign Policy (1963). *In his contribution to the present volume, Cohen explains where he thinks historians have erred in their assumptions about opinion and the policy making process.*

Alfred H. Kelly, who discusses Cohen's paper, is co-author of The American Constitution (1948), *and he has also worked in the field of American diplomatic history.*

The Relationship Between
Public Opinion and
Foreign Policy Maker

◆

Bernard C. Cohen

DEPARTMENT OF POLITICAL SCIENCE, UNIVERSITY OF WISCONSIN

I

FOREIGN POLICY IS quite obviously singled out from all other areas of public policy for special attention and study from the perspective of public opinion, and it is perhaps worthwhile to speculate, at the outset, why this is so. It seems to me to have its roots in two special characteristics of foreign policy. One is the disturbingly high costs and risks that are now associated with it; and the other is the fact that it seems to be peculiarly beyond our reach as policy-attentive and policy-active citizens. It is ironic, not to say frustrating, that groups of specially affected citizens seem to have ways of getting a grip on limited-impact issue-areas, such as agricultural policy or savings-and-loan regulations or auto safety standards, while the "really important questions" of war and peace, life and death, which belong to us all, seem to have eluded our grasp and to be in the hands of a higher and more mysterious imperative. The special academic interest in the impact of public opinion on the foreign policy maker stems thus from both a civic concern and a professional curiosity over the apparent intractability of foreign policy.

The search for understanding and explanation of the relationship between opinion and foreign policy making (which is implicitly also the search for better access to it) has been intense since World War II. It has also been fragmented, and if I may say so, generally not quite to the point of the question of impact. As a result of substantial research, we know quite a bit now about the nature and structure of opinions within the body politic on particular foreign policy issues, about their location in the political and social structure of the nation, and about the dynamics of their development and their change. We know a lot about interest groups, and a considerable amount about the press, as instruments for the presentation and circulation and advocacy of foreign policy views. We have done rather well, in other words, on almost every aspect of public opinion *up to* the point where the relationship with policy makers actually begins. But we know strikingly little, in an assured way, about the impact that the body of nongovernmental opinion has upon the men who formulate and execute American foreign policy—which is, I take it, the essence of the question that concerns us. To explore that relationship, we are of necessity led away from the source and character of the opinions themselves, and toward the objects of those opinions, the policy makers. We want to know, both in general terms and in specific cases, how public opinion widely defined actually bears upon the decisions they make.

To put the problem this way is to make abundantly clear the practical difficulties in our path. There are several ways to turn, to surmount them. One is to study foreign policy officials directly, to observe contemporaneously how nongovernmental opinion is factored into policy. Another and perhaps antecedent way is to examine the history of foreign policy issues—the case studies of foreign policy formulation—to see what they can tell us about the impact of nongovernmental opinions on prior foreign policy decisions. The central concern of this paper is with this latter mode of inquiry. We look to the historian for a larger sample of relevant cases from which to draw information and on which to base generalizations. What can we learn about the relationship between public opinion and foreign policy makers throughout the twentieth century that enlarges our present understanding and gives better focus to our contemporary concern?

The question as I have just formulated it is ambiguous, and deliberately so. The question "what can we learn?" can be answered in two ways: by a substantive interpretation of the opinion-policy relationship, drawn from the historical record itself; and by a literal, evaluative, answer that rests on the adequacy of that historical record. I shall try to answer it both ways—not just to stir up trouble, but because I have very large doubts about the essential accuracy of that record. My *operational* questions, then, are as follows: What kinds of generalizations do we have, or can we construct, concerning the relationship between public opinion and foreign policy makers in the twentieth century? What are these generalizations based on? How accurate or valid are they? What do we need to know in order to do a better job of explaining the opinion-policy relationship not only in the past but in the present and future as well?

II

The sheer volume of twentieth century American historiography makes it impossible to itemize in any detail and with statistical precision the generalizations its pages contain that deal with the connections between public opinion and foreign policy. The impressions of a non-historian, however, are that on the whole rather powerful political force has been attributed to general public opinion, to the press, and to political interest groups in the foreign policy field. Some examples are legendary in any event: that public opinion, whipped up by the "yellow press," swept a reluctant President and Congress into a war with Spain in 1898;[1] that the Kellogg-Briand pact of 1928 was the product of the grassroots, of the growing force of enlightened public opinion;[2] that public opinion, stimulated by Father Coughlin and the Hearst press, forced the Senate into a last-minute rejection of the resolution providing for United States adherence to the World Court in 1935;[3] that public opinion compelled President Franklin D. Roosevelt to back away from his proposal to "quarantine the aggressors" by imposing economic sanctions against Japan in 1937.[4] And in the interstices of these landmark events, American foreign policy makers are said to have been steadily directed by a timorous public opinion which chose neutrality over collective security.[5] The chronicle is not exclusively an inter-war one, either. In the post-World War II period, public opinion is generally reported, *inter alia,* to have forced an unwilling and precipitate demobilization in 1945 and 1946,[6] and to have prevented successive administrations from recognizing Communist China after 1949.[7]

I do not mean to suggest that all historians of this period advance these interpretations; indeed, we will have occasion later to mention some significant exceptions. But this is the thrust of the historical argument, the major theme of historians' overview of the twentieth century American experience in foreign affairs. Dexter Perkins provides an exceptionally vivid example of this in his brief essay on the very topic: "In a sense that is true in no such degree in other nations, American diplomatic action has been determined by the people. . . . Uninstructed though the average citizen may be in the facts of international life, he still has an opinion with regard to them. If he does not know, he thinks he knows. And the conviction on his part is one that cannot be disregarded. Nor do those who conduct our affairs in the main desire to disregard it."[8] Following the logic of this position, Perkins attributes a mysterious power to public opinion in specific cases. At the Washington Disarmament Conference of 1921–22, for example, he states that Secretary of State Hughes "secured that parity with the British which American opinion (for no very clear reason, it must be conceded) demanded." And at the same conference the United States gave up, "in the face of Japanese pressure, the right to fortify Guam and the Philippines. . . . No doubt, as was frequently maintained at the time, because of the state of American public opinion, it would have been impossible to secure funds for such fortification in any case." And again: "As early as 1925, eschewing the very cautious view of the matter expressed by Secretary Hughes, and responding, no doubt, to the pressure of powerful elements in American opinion, Secretary Kellogg permitted the United States to take part in the deliberations of the Preparatory Commission on Disarmament that assembled at Geneva."[9]

These are, I imagine, reasonably familiar arguments to most of us; they are part of the folklore of our time, a central element in the explanation of the vast tragedies that have swept the world in this century. Folly on so grand a scale needs to have its source in some ultimate authority; and in our secular democracy, public opinion has replaced the Gods or the Fates or the Kings as that authority.

III

Despite the fact that these historical interpretations and explanations come to us from men with impressive professional credentials, I am profoundly skeptical about their accuracy, their validity, their relevance—and I trust I am not alone in that sentiment. My skepticism has three roots:

(1) We are in rather substantial ignorance about the public opinion-foreign policy relationship that takes place in specific circumstances and on particular issues before our very eyes today, when "access" to government by scholars and journalists is as good as it has ever been, and when the techniques for assessing the state of public opinion and measuring its impact are no doubt better. We believe we know some *general* things about that relationship, but it has proved to be extraordinarily difficult, if not impossible, to trace the flow of public opinion influence in the development of specific foreign policies with any precision whatsoever. Given that simple yet enormous fact, I find it incredible on the face of it that the task of discovery was easier in the past, or even that the simple passage of time makes this extraordinarily complex relationship any easier to ascertain. In point of fact, reliable evidence bearing on the opinion-policy relationship, hard as it is to come by today, scarcely exists among the historical data of the first third of the century, when even the nature of public opinion had not yet become the subject of systematic scientific inquiry. We are at a loss today to state in reasonably accurate terms the impact of public opinion on something as visible and attention-getting as our policy toward Communist China since 1949; A. T. Steele, for example, asserts that public opinion has restrained successive administrations from a policy of recognition, but he also asserts the contrary—that the foreign policy situation itself restrained the policy makers. Given this fundamental uncertainty in the midst of a book on the subject that marshals large amounts of opinion information, I find it very difficult to accept without fundamental question a greater certainty that comes in the form of simple assertions based on much more fragmentary evidence.

In matters so little subject to documentary or empirical verification as these, it seems to me that sifted truth does not necessarily rise to the surface. What does rise rather more often is the interpretation of him who publishes first—or most! It is astonishing how easy it is for one interpretation to gain legendary stature, without challenge even from contemporaries who, while they may not "know" better in the true sense, at least suspect better. This has happened, for example, in the case of Roosevelt's quarantine speech, which we shall look at more closely below. And in our own day, both Theodore C. Sorensen and Arthur M. Schlesinger, Jr. have given historical credence, and thus sanction, to the notion expressed in an AIPO press release that there was a marked shift in public opinion in favor of the Nuclear Test Ban Treaty that helped to put the treaty over.[10] Given the high long-term support in public opinion polls for a test-ban treaty, there are some grounds for questioning the extent of such a shift in the first place, and even greater grounds—in the pages of Sorensen and Schlesinger alone—for questioning whether any manifestations of such a shift had anything to do with the policy outcome.

In short, the record of contemporary historians and analysts of public opinion does not warrant our putting much—or indeed any—confidence in the judgments of an earlier period that are based, unavoidably, on a selective reading of the press or on the accounts of one or at most a few observers or participants.

(2) A second reason for my skepticism about the validity of the conventional historical wisdom lies in the very improbability of its assertions, in the light of what little we do know about public opinion and foreign policy. One needs to repeat at this point that the literature of public opinion and public policy in general, and of public opinion and foreign policy in particular, largely evades the question of the relationship between opinion and policy; it has simply not been the focal point of study. But as I noted in (1) above, we nevertheless believe we know in *general* terms some things about that relationship in the contemporary United States. And what we have learned in diverse ways from diverse sources clearly suggests a foreign policy making establishment that is under very few public opinion constraints. And if these constraints are few in a period of substantial public attention to foreign policy questions, one cannot help asking why they should have been systematically and uniformly more extensive in an earlier period of our history, when there is no evidence that public attention was any greater than it is now, and lots of mythology suggesting that it was less.

Contemporary scholarship on public opinion and foreign policy repeatedly underlines the capacity of leaders to shape the public opinion to which they are supposedly responsive, and to interpret the opinions they hear in ways that support their own views. Gabriel Almond's classic study amply documented the foreign policy ignorance and disinterest of the great mass of the population even in the midst of the historic post-war "revolution" in American foreign policy, and the responsiveness of the small attentive segments of the population to the definitions of issues that emanate from the leadership groups.[11] My own study of the formulation of the Japanese peace settlement in the early 1950s revealed that in the general political-strategic aspects of foreign policy, the administration had a virtually free hand; it was only in dealing with Pacific Ocean fisheries questions that foreign policy makers ran into a constituency that had a sufficiently direct interest in the outcome to warrant active and effective—and congressionally supported—involvement.[12] The study of reciprocal trade renewal by Bauer, Pool and Dexter illuminates in a variety of ways the political and perceptual screens used by officials (in this case, congressmen) to filter public responses so that they hear chiefly what they want to hear, thus attenuating the impact of public opinion even on an issue of economic foreign policy—the very issue-area that has seemed to be the most responsive in the foreign policy field to nongovernmental influence.[13]

The President is especially powerful as a shaper of public opinion, since he is the acknowledged symbol of and spokesman for the country in foreign affairs. He commands attention from the media whenever he wants it, he formulates policy alternatives with an authority that no one else possesses, and he has a substantial and more or less natural base of sympathy and identification on which he can draw and which he can dissipate only with the greatest difficulty. Every major crisis in American foreign policy in the last generation, including those for which responsibility lies at the door of the White House, such as the U-2 incident and the Bay of Pigs, has been followed by an upsurge in popular support for the President.[14] According to Sorensen, Kennedy clearly understood the freedom that his position gave him: "The final difference in the Kennedy treatment of foreign and domestic affairs was the relative influence of Congressional and public opinion. His foreign policy actions were still constrained within bounds set by those forces, but they operated more indirectly than directly and his own powers of initiative and decision were much wider."[15]

Given the conditions that seem to account for this situation—substantial public disinterest, the expectation of executive authority and initiative, the capacity of the President to be a focal point in the public discussion of foreign policy—it seems reasonable to believe that the same situation would hold at least for the major foreign policy questions of the earlier period in the twentieth century. And for all issues defined as "minor," meaning that they did not heavily engage the interest and energy of the political system, it is at least as reasonable to believe that the President and the secretary of state had no incentive to bend with the pale breezes of special interest as to believe that they had no strength to resist them. On the very face of it, for example, it seems highly improbable that so imprecise, so divided, and so superficial a political force as public opinion could have compelled President Franklin Roosevelt to retreat overnight from his public statement on quarantining aggressors. "Retreat" he may have, at least to the extent of not repeating the suggestion of a quarantine —but the ordinary short-term indicators of public opinion, especially editorial reaction, White House mail, and interest group stands, were on his side, and so substantially as to strengthen one's doubts that it was the united impact or even the majority of nongovernmental opinion that moved him.[16]

(3) My third reason for being skeptical about the conventional historical wisdom concerning public opinion and foreign policy is more prosaic, if more fundamental: much of the existing literature, the very basis for the historical judgment as well as the expression of it, simply does not handle public opinion convincingly, no matter what conclusions it comes to about public opinion as a political force. The vast bulk of the literature makes no attempt systematically to prove or disprove a causal relationship between opinion and policy, or even to investigate so simple a proposition as that an observed convergence between opinion and policy may be attributable more to the fluidity of opinion than to the mobility of policy, or alternatively that such a convergence may be the result of independent responses to the same political stimuli. No exhaustive review of the literature is possible here, but two examples may illustrate the inadequacies of the record that weaken one's confidence in it.

Robert Browder's study of the circumstances leading up to the U.S. recognition of the U.S.S.R. attempts to put a major shift in U.S. foreign policy into a broad public, political and economic context; his conclusion is that the desire for expanded trade did not play the paramount role in American recognition of the Soviet Union, that the arguments for increased trade were a convenient cover making a diplomatic enterprise palatable to public opinion. But his arguments about public opinion, as distinct from his conclusion, are inconsistent, contradictory, and unsupported by his evidence. He repeatedly presents the public statements and positions of individuals on the recognition question parallel to the views of policy makers, with the clear implication—but not the evidence—that they were strongly felt, even where they were ignored. I find it hard to fault Browder on his key observations that President Hoover was determined *not* to recognize the Soviet Union no matter how much agitation he encountered from business groups, and that President Roosevelt came to office equally determined to normalize diplomatic relations with the U.S.S.R. no matter what.[17] But fault him or not, it is hard to give equal credence on the one hand to assertions that Roosevelt was from the very beginning determined to alter an anomalous situation, and on the other hand to statements such as, "Among all the other facts which Roosevelt had taken into account before he sent his historic invitation to Kalinin, none perhaps was more instrumental in deciding him to act when he did than his realization that American public opinion in the main supported a resumption of relations with Russia."[18] And it is also difficult to give equal credence both to the latter observation, and to the repeated references throughout the book to American public opinion as isolationist, anti-Communist, fearful of "international complications," so much so that one could not speak openly of political reasoning or advantage.[19] If one took Browder's generalizations about public opinion at face value, one would have to conclude that recognition could never have taken place.

Steele's study, *The American People and China,* cited earlier, shares these defects of analysis and interpretation of public opinion. On the one hand, Steele argues that Congress and the Executive continue to be immobilized on China policy because the mail, editorial opinion, public opinion soundings, and pressure group activity are all ranged against any change, any softening, in our policy toward Peking. "As one author observes, 'A large part of the history of American foreign policy since World War I might be interpreted as a series of successful intimidations by pressure groups.' The applicability of this statement to the China situation is self-evident."[20] And again, in referring to the hostility of the China lobby and its successor groups, supported even by more respectable national organizations, he states: "Members of Congress are of course well aware of this powerful body of opinion and of the hardened attitude of a large and influential section of the popular press. They consciously or subconsciously take it into consideration in weighing any legislation that involves a change in our relations with Communist countries."[21]

On the other hand, Steele repeatedly acknowledges, as a kind of afterthought, that any reconsideration of our China policy "is of course inhibited also by the Peking regime's chronic truculence."[22] In other words, he argues that the Chinese situation itself offers the United States no reasonable alternative to its present policy. Policy is substantially frozen because very few people, inside the government or outside, think that the prospects for change are bright enough to justify much effort or great risk. U.S. policy thus is very largely a response not to internal opinion pressures but to an international political situation over which, in the short run at least, this country has little control. The ambivalence and confusion in Steele's argument concerning the responsibility of public opinion for our present China policy is well illustrated by the following. While he continues to assert that policy makers in Congress and the executive branch live in fear of hostile public reactions if they so much as mention a reappraisal of our China policy, he also notes that the speech by Assistant Secretary of State Hilsman in December 1963, which held open the door to better relations with the next echelon or generation of Chinese leaders, was initiated in the State Department and was favorably received by the American press—though not by the Chinese! In this case, as in the matter of the recognition of the Soviet Union, it is next to impossible to draw firm conclusions about the actual constraints imposed on policy makers by public opinion; and these two studies are better informed about the public opinion dimension than are most historical narratives.

IV

One can understand how an individual might be misled in the process of trying to reconstruct a single and specific decision; but—assuming there is validity in my rather sweeping criticism—how is one to account for such a general misunderstanding or misinterpretation of the impact of public opinion on foreign policy making? What is wrong with our capacity to understand the processes of foreign policy formulation? Why do contemporary scholars persist in attributing great political force to nongovernmental opinions in the foreign policy field in the absence of direct evidence and when almost everything we know about public opinion and foreign policy, both of a specific and a general character, indicates the contrary? At the risk of oversimplification, a few likely causes can be explored, especially because it is in these possible causes that we may find good guidelines to a more accurate and thus more relevant historiography of foreign policy making.

There seems, in the first instance, to be a general intellectual failure, a failure of political conceptualization or theoretical insight on a grand scale. We are all familiar with the principles of normative democratic theory concerning public opinion; and we have long lacked good empirical theories or even descriptive propositions about the foreign policy making process. As one way out of this difficulty, we have apparently been willing to accept normative theories in explanation of what has happened in specific instances for which we have had no other satisfactory or compelling mode of explanation. Another way of accommodating the normatively derived power of public opinion to concrete situations that are devoid of supporting evidence has been to assert that public opinion is indeed powerful, but at the edges of policy rather than at the center; thus public opinion "sets the boundaries" within which foreign policy operates and—implicitly—beyond which it cannot or must not go. This notion sometimes appears explicitly in the literature of explanation, and it is so common as a general consideration that it could hardly fail to be an implicit factor in conceptualizations of foreign policy making in concrete circumstances. The trouble with this notion is that it can only be taken on faith, never proved or disproved, because the "boundaries" of policy are in principle unknown and undefinable. In practice, however, they can only be defined by the things that policy makers have already *chosen* to do or not to do; and thus to say that public opinion sets those boundaries is in fact to attribute a central role in all policy to public opinion, which is manifestly neither intended as a statement nor true as a fact.

The lack of comprehensive empirically based hypotheses about foreign policy making has also, I believe, given longer life to what we might call the Lippmann fallacy: the view that political executives are the repositories of foreign policy initiative and intelligence (in both senses), and that the mass publics in twentieth century western democracies are the sources of unreasoned restraint, negativism, short-run escape from responsibility and commitment, whether through evasion or its opposite, over-response.[23] In combination, all of these intellectual and conceptual weaknesses have created a predisposition to believe that, where there was no other ready explanation for foreign policy behavior that did not fit some preconceived and generally implicit notion of political rationality, the deviation must have been caused by public opinion in some manifestation.

These conceptual failures have been sustained and even nourished by statements of policy makers themselves. I appreciate the fact that official pronouncements, and observations and recollections of officials, have a special claim to historical relevance, particularly when other sources of evidence are not readily found. But it is precisely the importance that we are obliged to attach to such statements that should compel us to look at them with a cold and fishy eye, and to ask of them, as we have asked of the historians' accounts, are they reasonable or verifiable? For example, Herbert Feis, an official-turned-historian, wrote the following in partial explanation of the state department's failure to give firm support to League of Nations sanctions against Italy in the Italian-Ethiopian War: "There was in the Department a thin hope . . . that public opinion might finally awaken to what was at issue, and demand further and more decisive action. This hope, however, fed largely upon itself. Officials could not find, either in the mail received at the State Department or in the press, evidence that public opinion was insistent upon more vigorous control of trade with Italy."[24] It seems to me quite unreasonable to claim that officials failed to take "more decisive action" because public opinion did not demand or insist on it; since when has this been the source of initiative in foreign policy?

We are accustomed to being told by our secretaries of state that public opinion shapes foreign policy, that the policy maker is guided by public sentiment, and so forth. One would expect the secretary of state to say such things, if only because he believes they are expected of him; this is, after all, what the most articulate members of his nongovernmental audience really want to hear (though the few I know do not believe it either!). But there are other, more proximate and practical reasons why officials talk this way, which I believe really account for the unreliability of their statements. When a policy maker is attributing a decision to the dictates of public opinion, he is explaining away a variety of complicated, delicate political constraints on his and his colleagues' behavior by passing them off onto the one legitimate political actor that cannot answer back, defend itself, or take offense at the charge. He may have been led to a particular policy step because it was the only action on which he could get any agreement from the interested parties within the state department or the executive branch; or he may have concluded *not* to do something by the clear, if unpublicized, intimation of congressional reprisal, or even because he himself was unwilling to shoulder responsibility for all the risks involved. To explain his decision by blaming himself or his colleagues or Congress would be most unwise; but to lay it all on the shoulders of the public might even be construed as flattering. I do not believe, incidentally, that this is a conscious and deliberate subterfuge; rather, it seems to me to be so automatic a set of euphemisms and rationalizations that it constitutes an institutionalized response to the felt necessity of saying something about ultimate responsibility for decisions, wise or unwise.

The heart of the intellectual failure—and a strong reason why it has been so easy for statesmen to get away with patently absurd remarks—is the absence of theories of foreign policy making based on a realistic understanding of political strategies. For reasons that can be explained if not justified, foreign policy as a subject matter has been treated as a special thing in American political science, substantially divorced from the theories and concepts of the political process that specialists in American politics have developed. Even in American government textbooks, foreign policy is invariably treated, in two or three chapters at the end, as a major *problem area* of American government, and not as a major set of questions and issues that define, shape and illustrate the very way the American government and American politics operate. Thus, while there are now some rather elaborate theories of the political process in areas such as budget making or military policy, for example, foreign policy still appears as a subject that is more appropriately studied from the point of view of international politics than of national politics. This blindness to the political strategies of foreign policy making is no doubt largely a function of the fact that much of the foreign policy making process is invisible to the casual observer, being carried on within the confines of the executive branch and often under the wraps of national security, and that Congress has less of a role to play in comparison with areas of domestic policy. Public opinion, and nongovernmental actors generally, have tended consequently to be conceived of as operating more or less directly on the foreign policy officials, rather than more subtly being engaged in a complex political process that envelops large sections of the national political system. One result of this primitive theory of foreign policy making is that it is a contest between "good guys" and "bad guys," the latter being not those in dark shirts but all the unenlightened people on the outside who presumably impede rational policies.

Before we can ever get a reliable statement of the relationship between public opinion and foreign policy maker, we need a fuller and more accurate set of propositions about the larger political processes of foreign policy making, of which public opinion is just a part. And, more narrowly but equally important, we need to know what the expressions of public opinion look like, not to the historian or the contemporary observer or even the persons who articulate them, but to the foreign policy officials themselves. On this point the evidence from history is very poor indeed; scholars have not often looked for it, and when they have it has been more suggestive than conclusive. But we have good reason to believe that an official's perception of public opinion on foreign policy questions differs substantially from the perceptions that others are likely to have.[25] So it is of more than idle curiosity that we learn how policy makers actually do perceive their total environment, including their opinion environment, in specific cases.

It is not beyond reason to speculate that throughout the twentieth century foreign policy leaders have not generally known how free they were to pursue policies in which they were interested. On an earlier occasion I summarized it as follows: "Seeing, in a shadowy way, chiefly the restrictive elements in a probable political process, the policy-maker often spins around himself an artificial web of constraint."[26] Impressions from the historical literature suggest the proposition that policy makers are as often surprised by the lack of public response to what they have done as they are by the nature of responses that do occur. By way of illustration, Browder depicts Roosevelt as having been determined to proceed with the recognition of the Soviet Union despite an articulate body of opinion that opposed the move; but in the aftermath he concludes that "the volume of protest was evidently considerably less than the Administration had anticipated."[27] Brzezinski and Huntington, in their comparison of the American and Soviet political systems, observe that in the United States post-hoc criticisms of foreign policy "certainly shape the Administration's anticipations of the reactions to its next decision in the same area and thereby also presumably affect the content of that decision."[28] To the extent that administrations do approach new decisions in this fashion, having public reactions to the last decisions uppermost in mind, it is not surprising that they may often be surprised when the expected responses do not materialize.

I do not believe that it is inconsistent to argue, however, that even though foreign policy leaders have widely underestimated their freedom of maneuver in foreign policy, they still perceive that freedom more accurately than many scholars have, and more accurately even than they themselves usually admit openly. Joseph M. Jones' description of the development of the Truman Doctrine and the Marshall Plan is noteworthy for its recognition that the foreign policy leaders had to take the initiative all the way, and that the public had to be "educated" to support the grand venture.[29] H. Schuyler Foster, for many years chief of the State Department's office of public opinion studies, has asserted that on the Truman Doctrine, as on a large number of important foreign policy questions of the period, both the executive and Congress had no hesitation in acting without public approval and support—that public responsiveness has followed in due course.[30] And while Secretary of State Rusk talks about the public limitations on foreign policy, Sorensen writes about Kennedy's clear understanding that, of the various foreign policy constraints he faced, this one was marginal.[31] Furthermore, my own research in the public opinion perceptions of state department officials persuades me that most of their talk about the power of public opinion is ritualistic; when one probes its meaning, it usually either disappears entirely, or transmutes into something else, like congressional politics. In either case, the officials themselves are not deceived by the words they use into believing that their hands are tied by nongovernmental opinions.

We need, finally, a substantial reexamination of the history of American foreign policy making in the twentieth century, along with better studies of contemporary foreign policy making. This should not be read as a call for historical revisionism that makes new and different interpretations with no more substantial evidence than before. Rather, it is a request for systematic and focused attention, in historical research, to such questions as these. In specific situations in the past, what is the best evidence concerning policy makers' perceptions of the domestic policy making environment, including the public opinion environment? And what specific modifications or constraints were *thereby* imposed on their foreign policy preferences or intentions? There are some good historical models that demonstrate what can be done by asking relevant questions of an admittedly imperfect and even intractable body of evidence. George W. Auxier, for example, has questioned the significance of sensational journalism in the events leading up to the Spanish-American War, by examining the press in the Midwest, where the Hearst-Pulitzer circulation war did not reach. He has concluded that to the extent that the press played a part in the development of a war policy, it was more likely the result of press consideration of questions of national interest and of political partisanship, rather than sensational, circulation-induced demands for intervention.[32] And in her impressive study of President Roosevelt and the Quarantine Speech, Dorothy Borg has explored his apparent intentions, the public reactions to the speech, and his perceptions of those reactions; and she has concluded that Roosevelt had no specific sanctions in mind from which he was dissuaded, and that there was quite extensive and respectable public support for his speech, but that so far as future policy was concerned, he was extraordinarily sensitive to the isolationist and pacifist segments of that public opinion (which had resonance in the views of leading senators) rather than to the broad supportive sections of public opinion.[33] One wonders what a comparably insightful study of, for example, the political predispositions of senators and their exposure to lobbying activities against U.S. entry into the World Court, set into the larger political context and issue context of the day, would conclude about the true causes for the rejection of U.S. membership. A large variety of such studies, better informed by better hypotheses about the political processes of foreign policy making, would make a substantial contribution to our understanding of the public opinion-foreign policy making relationship across the twentieth century to the present day.

Comment 3

◆

Alfred H. Kelly

DEPARTMENT OF HISTORY, WAYNE STATE UNIVERSITY

LET ME SAY at the outset that I have a very considerable degree of sympathy with large portions of Cohen's paper. Professional loyalties in academia are generally so narrow and unimaginative as to subject any historian who agrees even in part with strictures levelled by a political scientist against his craft to a charge of high treason. But it is difficult not to agree with Cohen's point that a great deal of what has passed for proven causal relationships between public opinion and policy making in diplomatic history has in fact been little more than "a myth agreed upon by historians." Or as Cohen puts it, it is the "interpretation of him who publishes first—or most" which wins general acceptance and finds its way into the textbooks and other manifestations of "orthodox" historical thinking about the past.

A cynic might observe at this point that a goodly portion of contemporary scholarly activity in the field of diplomatic history consists of challenging a great variety of long established causal interpretations. In fact, this has become of late years the accepted manner in which young historians strive to win professional attention. Their new ideas will in time achieve a certain degree of orthodoxy, and thus become the point of departure for still another generation of aspiring young scholars seeking to validate their academic credentials with their elders. Perhaps, therefore, we ought to close ranks against any "outsider" who challenges the adequacy of the traditional processes of historical scholarship, lest the foundations of the academic temple tremble. Unfortunately for professional integrity of the narrow sort, however, Cohen's ideas are important, even if not altogether original among historians. They undoubtedly deserve some considerable attention and analysis.

Although Cohen does not state the matter precisely in so many words, the nub of his criticism of diplomatic historians and their generalizations about the role of public opinion lies in an implied attack on historical methodology. The four or five initial examples he gives of doubtful, unproven, or "legendary" causal relationships between public opinion and the formulation of public policy—from the Spanish-American war to Roosevelt's failure to follow through on the implications of his quarantine speech—are in every instance examples that illustrate the defective fashion in which historians at large all too often arrive at the truth.

Briefly, historical truth seeking may be described somewhat as follows. The historian who undertakes to examine a particular complex of events in the past will be struck first of all by the vast and overwhelming sea of factual detail which confronts him, much or most of it without any apparent inner consistency or order. But at this point the historian's professional training asserts itself—he is under a powerful compulsion to bring order out of chaos by constructing a model of some sort. Furthermore it no longer suffices, as it once did the chronicler of the Icelandic sagas, merely to impose a time sequence order upon the historian's view of factual detail. Mere historical narrative no longer will do. Instead, an objective imposed by analogy from the exact sciences controls historical research. The historian must seek not only to impose a narrative order but also a sequential causal order upon his mass of data. And it is at precisely this point that he gets into trouble, for his profession has equipped him with almost no tools of any sophistication for undertaking this process.

This historian's difficulty with the problem of causation has its root in a fact obvious to all members of our craft—the techniques for ascertaining causal relationship, which are appropriate to the physicist, the biologist, or indeed even to the psychologist and sociologist, are not available to him. For the essence of research in all these fields is the isolation of a body of repetitive data of a standardized kind whose characteristics, once isolated, can be subjected to mathematical analysis. Even in the social sciences, where standardized repetitive data often are more difficult to arrive at—as for example in political science—there are still important areas where research can be subsumed under the rubric of data gathering, subjecting data to comparative analysis through the control-group techniques, and then describing the results statistically with a result which to some extent at least approaches the formulation of social "law." Laws so derived are nearly always stated in "causal" form; that is, when *A* occurs it will, according to a certain process, be followed by *B*. This process may be reduced finally to one of statistical probability or statistical correlation, which is merely one way of expressing causation mathematically.

Unfortunately for the historian, none of all this—or almost none of it —can as a rule be applied to his craft. For the essence of any given historical situation lies in its uniqueness—that is, its nonrepetitive quality. To cite one of Cohen's examples, the story of the origins and evolution of the Kellogg-Briand pact is, from a historian's point of view, absolutely unique. Indeed, the historian is likely to insist that it is the very unique- ness of the complex of events in question that makes the event worth- while for the diplomatic historian. A political scientist might reply in turn that there may be standardized elements in the Kellogg-Briand situation which are subject to extrapolation and to statistical causal analysis, the results of which might be subsumed in some kind of fundamental statement of an abstract kind about the relationship between public opinion and foreign policy. But to this the historian might give what for him is a final rejoinder: all this may be true enough, but that he remains interested in the peculiar aggregate of happenings surrounding the emer- gence of the Kellogg-Briand pact, and that it is this peculiar and unique aggregate of facts which gives the event its significance for him.

And so we have the historian's dilemma. For him all events are unique, and conversely he is traditionally interested primarily in the uniqueness of events, not their universality. But this means he runs into trouble on Hume's traditional concept of causation. The reader will remember that Hume described causation merely as the process whereby, if event *A* occurred, it was invariably followed by event *B*. Hume thought it was not possible to describe causal relationship otherwise. A modern exact scientist might be a little more sophisticated. He would say that when event *A* occurs, then event *B* probably occurs; then *A* may be said to "cause" *B*. "If *A,* then probably *B*." The relationship in modern terms then becomes one, as observed above, of statistical correlation, expressed with mathematical exactitude. But if events A and B are both unique and nonrecurrent, how can the concept of "if A, probably B" apply? The answer is simple; it cannot.

This does not mean that the historian is absolutely estopped from using the concept of causation, but the nature of his craft does impose severe limits upon his technique. For example, if in considering the possible causal relationship between A and B, it can be shown that A is a fictitious event—a nonevent, if you will—then the historian is safe in saying that A did not cause B. Observe, by the way, that one or two of Cohen's examples fall in this category. If for example, an examination of the background of public opinion, as measured by the common historical indices of the time, indicates that public interest in a general pact outlawing war was absent or virtually absent in 1927–1928, then it becomes clear that public opinion did not inspire or "cause" the pact to come into being; A in our formula did not exist.

Again, if the historian can show that not only did A exist in relation to B but that A' and A'' also existed prior to B, then he can express profound skepticism about the relationship of A and B. This is Cohen's case with respect to the background of public opinion and the Spanish-American war. The Hearst and Pulitzer press were indeed having a circulation war in the years 1896–1898. Both newspaper chains did exploit the Cuban insurrection for circulation purposes. (Taken together, these equal event A.) The war then did occur in 1898. By the traditional accepted formula as stated by Bailey and others, the inflammation of public opinion (A in our formula) caused the outbreak of war (B). But the Auxier article cited by Cohen throws doubt upon the uniqueness of A in relation to B by showing that various midwestern papers not affected by the Hearst-Pulitzer circulation war also were advocating a war policy, although in a different spirit and apparently for differing motives. Enter A, A' and A''; that is, the concept of multiple causation. The unique relation of A to B is thereby destroyed. It becomes "untrue" for the historian to say simply that the Hearst-Pulitzer circulation fight so inflamed public opinion that it "caused" the McKinley administration to start the war.

But most of the time the diplomatic historian's lot, like that of his fellow craftsmen, is not such a happy one. How, then, does he solve his problem? He has infinite facts, which a little creative imagination then polarizes around a series of major events. He then engages in model building, based in fact upon a series of half-conscious and generally unstated assumptions about the nature of the underlying social forces he is dealing with. A causal model presently makes its appearance; indeed once the unconscious assumptions are put to work, the causal model in question fairly cries out in its demand for acceptance. From there it finds its way into scholarly literature, and if the model in question is in general accordance with the prevailing academic Weltanschauung—that is, a series of half-spoken presumptions about the nature of reality—then it will pass into professional literature and win general acceptance as the ortho-dox interpretation. That is in fact the origin of several of the models Cohen cites.

Cohen rests his skepticism about the public opinion–foreign policy models which diplomatic historians have commonly adopted upon three major grounds. First, he cites the incredible complexity of known foreign policy situations of our own time, points out how exceedingly difficult it is to factor out all the separate causal elements, including those of public opinion, and then by analogy concludes that those of the past seventy years probably have been vastly simplified by the historians who have set up simple causal models. In my opinion, Cohen has all the best of the argument here.

Second, Cohen expresses great skepticism about the general impact of public opinion upon foreign policy situations at large, stating that evidence "from diverse sources clearly suggests a foreign policy making establishment that is under very few public opinion constraints." And finally, he challenges the historian's techniques for handling public opinion and foreign policy, asserting once again in effect not only that historians lack adequate scientific techniques for ascertaining and analyzing the impact of public opinion, but also that diplomatic historians have been far too prone to assign a greater weight to the impact of public opinion than is justified generally by a careful evaluation of the available evidence.

The implication of Cohen's second and third point, it seems to me, is that the making of foreign policy is still very much the same self-contained process that it was in the days of Talleyrand, Castlereagh and Canning. I agree, and indeed I would argue that there is in fact an essentially nondemocratic or even indeed an aristocratic element about foreign policy which removes it to some degree from the ordinary party and parliamentary processes of democracy. Cohen doubtless would object to the word "aristocratic" as having class implications he could not accept, but he nonetheless does seem to be saying that foreign policy is not amenable to the impact of the democratic process to the same degree that internal political issues are. Astute Presidents, he says in effect, have recognized this. As did Roosevelt in recognizing Russia in 1933 and Kennedy in the Bay of Pigs crisis, they have acted out their convictions in the confident expectation that public opinion will then follow after them, like John Quincy Adams' famous cockboat, this time in the wake of enlightened executive leadership.

One can agree with this general argument but recognize that a basic question nonetheless remains: ought the impact of public opinion on foreign policy to be denigrated as far as Cohen believes? Have Dexter Perkins and other diplomatic historians been fundamentally wrong in assigning so large a role to the impact of public opinion on policy making?

Here I venture to suggest that Cohen has stated his argument for "self-containment" in foreign policy somewhat too strongly, and that the impact of public opinion on foreign policy making is of considerably more importance than he thinks. (My techniques for so concluding, by the way, are no more "scientific" than those of other diplomatic historians, or of Cohen in arguing his point.)

In the first place, it seems to me that Cohen picks and chooses his evidence of "minimum impact" for public opinion a little too carefully and selectively. Not only does he ignore certain rather notable situations in American history where it might be said that public opinion did unquestionably play an important role, he also is open to some challenge with respect to one or two of the public opinion–foreign policy situations he actually cites. I would tentatively argue, for example, that the force of public opinion brought to bear upon Congress in the summer and fall of 1939 was important both in the defeat of the bill to modify the third neutrality act and in the successful passage of the fourth neutrality act in November of that year. Again, for example, I believe also that Roosevelt had both ears to the ground—a feat an astute politician can occasionally accomplish—when he nursed interventionist sentiment along in the fall of 1940 on into the spring of 1941. Apparently believing American intervention in the war against Hitler to be inevitable, he nonetheless took extreme care, against the advice of several of his advisors, not to get "too far out in front" of public opinion.

I believe also that Cohen assesses Browder's work on American-Soviet relations less than fairly when in effect he accuses him of handling the evidence on Hoover's and F.D.R.'s recognition policies in a contradictory fashion. Apparently, Cohen thinks that because Hoover was determined not to recognize Russia, regardless of business pressure, and that F.D.R. presumably was determined to recognize, and presently did so, proves the point that public opinion was not important in either instance. I read the same evidence somewhat differently. Pressure for recognition was building up steadily after 1929 for a variety of reasons, some of them having to do with the changing state of public opinion toward the Soviet Union. Hoover successfully held out against this pressure, as he did in a great many like situations, both foreign and domestic, with political consequences for his administration which are only too well known. Roosevelt, by contrast, capitalized on the drift of public opinion to accomplish what he wanted. In fact, he encountered almost no public opinion opposition at all, which may very well be why he acted as quickly and decisively as he did. To resort to Humean skepticism once more, it is in fact not possible to prove the point either way.

Cohen thinks that policy makers often cite "public opinion" as a reason for acting or not acting, when in fact they may have been inspired or inhibited by other political factors which it may not be politic to discuss publicly. Agreed. But I suggest there is a considerable body of evidence to indicate that public opinion today is factored into the formula with respect to any given foreign policy consideration more prominently than in Castlereagh's time—both in the United States and in other modern constitutional states in the state system.

In a thoughtful article Franz Schnabel has argued that indeed the rise of public opinion as a factor in foreign policy making in the last hundred years has altered permanently the nature of the diplomatic process.[34] I suspect this is true. As a single example of the evidence on the point, I would appeal to Ernest R. May's careful study of the process of internal policy making in Germany, England and America during World War I, which shows quite decisively the important role public opinion, particularly as brought to bear through the party process, played in the crucial decisions taken by those in power in all three states with respect to peace and war.[35]

There is a related point involved here—the extent to which the authors of foreign policy genuinely believe that public opinion is a significant factor in their ability to control the making of foreign policy. Since the days of Napoleon and *Le Moniteur,* I would argue, heads of state have been convinced of the necessity for having a favorable public opinion behind them, and have sought to obtain that result, whether or not a favorable public opinion was in fact as essential to their freedom of maneuver as they thought it was. What Presidents and secretaries of state have *thought* about the role of public opinion as brought to bear upon the organs of policy making is something that can be documented, quite apart from mere speculation about possible causal relationships. And many Presidents—from Polk and his war message of 1846, which appealed to the all-important myth of self-defense, to Franklin Roosevelt and his foreign policy fireside chats—have made clear their conviction that public opinion is something to be taken into account. It will not do to say that they sometimes acted against public opinion. Of course they did. But they also took it into account as a factor—and an important factor—in analyzing the potentials for policy in any given situation where crucial decisions had to be forthcoming.

Finally, at issue behind the overt assumptions of Cohen's paper, at last, is the question of whether or not we live in an essentially revolutionary age. I believe we do, and that this means there is an important element of "discontinuity" between our age and earlier periods—even those of fifty or seventy-five years ago—as to the factors which make up the foreign policy formula for modern constitutional states. If this is true, then examples drawn from diplomatic history may be to some extent obsolete, and we may be in a period in which historians and political scientists may be obliged to draw new causal generalizations about the aggregate of public opinion and pressure factors in present day foreign policy making. The idea is not a pleasant one for a historian to entertain; in fact, like the opening statements of this paper about historians and the problem of causation, the notion of discontinuity may have within it an element of outright treason to the craft. But we can afford to be generous; the historian's profession appears to have a kind of odor of absolute legitimacy about it, even in a revolutionary age.

4

Once the historian has satisfactorily established that public opinion does play some role in the policy making process, he must then move on to the difficult task of defining or isolating those factors which affect opinion. As noted above, the diplomatic historian often relies exclusively upon the most prosaic of sources, the newspaper or magazine editorial. At the same time, psychologists and sociologists have demonstrated that editorials are among the least influential molders of public opinion.

In Scratches on Our Minds *(1958) Harold R. Isaacs explored American images of China and India in the late fifties. Although he was concerned more with the images than their purveyors, he did call attention to the incredible variety of sources which influenced our Asian experts' perceptions. In this paper Isaacs returns to that earlier research, but this time with an emphasis upon sources.*

Athan Theoharis, who evaluates the paper, is a specialist in recent American history and has written The Yalta Myths *(1970), a study of the wartime conference as a political issue during the cold war.*

Sources for Images of
Foreign Countries

Harold R. Isaacs

CENTER FOR INTERNATIONAL STUDIES,
MASSACHUSETTS INSTITUTE OF TECHNOLOGY

OUR DISCUSSION HERE has supplied us with some apt images with which to picture ourselves. We have been told about the sea of myths in which everyone is floating. Much has been made of what each one of us sees when we look at the scene outside that window. We have also been given a picture of sales-resistant historians skeptically looking over the show-cases of social science, barely fingering and certainly not buying its varied wares. We have also had some living evidence that there are still histori-ans who seriously believe they practice a discipline which fills *their* showcases with nothing but whole and consistent and polyunsaturated truths. These are metaphors which beg for mixing and I cannot refrain from asking you to think of all the historians who have looked out of all their many windows, and of the great and untidily crowded supermarket of varieties of what they have seen out there, depending on the particular spot in the sea of myths in which each one happened to be floating at his particular time.

We have also been exposed here to the implication—so often made by social scientists talking to humanists—that social science has produced a much more systematic body of knowledge about human affairs, a measur-able objectivity much more rigorously obtained, and that if only members of less rigorous disciplines (or members of the government, the press, or the public) would look through that window with *their* social scientific eyes, chaos would yield more or less magically to order. But I think the evidence, reproduced again in this one small group in this one small room, has shown that we are all floundering about in that sea of myths, each one clinging hard to the one bit or piece of knowledge he feels he has and struggling not to be struck or swamped by all the other flotsam and jetsam around him. As professional intellectuals, historians and social scientists may paddle around a bit more purposively, and sometimes, by clearing some slightly larger area around them, might come to imagine their own little pools are the whole sea. But of course they never are. What each one of us sees depends on where each one is looking from, and when, and what the light is, and what the obstructions are, either in his external line of vision or in his own mind. As most serious hard scientists now acknowledge—it seems to come harder from the softer kinds—all observation is subject to the observer, and to the time, place, and circumstances in which it takes place.

In the affairs that concern us—human affairs and behavior—these include the familiar categories of national, class, caste or other special interest. Less familiarly, they also include the assumptions, myths, perceptions of both the observer and the observed, the predispositions, prejudices, and biases, the pictures in our heads which Walter Lippmann began trying to call to our attention so long ago, the images-of-others and images-of-self that every person carries around with him and that shape what he sees, feels, thinks about himself, his group, other groups, or the human condition in general. This is true of us all, of the historian trying to reconstruct the past, the social scientist trying to order the present, the policy maker or opinion shaper trying to direct events, or plain everyman with his head through the canvas, the object and target of it all. Each one has been conditioned—programmed would now be the apter word—from infancy to make him what he is, to think what he thinks, to see the world in the light and shape that he sees it, to do what he does. What we see when we look at history or society is the enlargement of these pictures in these many heads projected onto the larger screens that surround us—and we see them through the prisms of our own minds, the shapes of the pictures in our own heads. The search for greater rigor, for a better grasp on reality, a wider view of the scene, has to begin with an awareness of what these pictures are and how they have been acquired. And this must begin with the pictures in the head of the searcher himself, for the truth is, I believe, that every such search, like all art, is autobiographical.

This leaves us at best on a spongy atoll or a slippery rock, for as all good historians and social scientists must know, evidence can usually be assembled to make myths out of anyone's truth, and the psychiatrists complicate the matter still further by making truths out of everyone's myths. But however precarious the footing, since my proposition is that our views of history are to a major extent determined by our individual exposures, I shall offer no apologies for pursuing the matter here with some autobiographical notes of my own that begin to illustrate my point.

On the night of April 12, 1927, I was riding in a taxicab in midtown Manhattan, not yet seventeen, out on one of my first dates—I was a freshman at Columbia, the girl a freshman at Barnard. As we came out of the canyons at 59th Street into the open space where Central Park begins, we came full onto a view of a spectacular fire. The scaffolding around the top of the new Sherry Netherlands Hotel over on Fifth Avenue was ablaze, burning like a great torch nearly forty stories high in the sky. The girl and fire were cause enough to make the date memorable—but I mean the date with the girl, not the date April 12, 1927. Seven years later my wife—the same girl—and I were in Peking combing libraries and newspaper files for material on the events of the Chinese revolution of the previous decade. Among them, we had come to know, the date of April 12, 1927, stood starkly high. It was the day of Chiang Kai-shek's coup d'etat in Shanghai, when he turned against his Communist allies and began in the streets of the city the mass slaughters that continued for months thereafter wherever his control was established. It was the climactic event in the whole affair. In the process of checking out every account we could find of that day's happenings, my wife went through a file of the *New York Times,* which we found in the Peking Language School Library, and there on the lead side of the front page of the issue of April 13, 1927, was a large picture of that flaming hotel tower. Opposite, on the left-hand side in the corresponding top position under a two-column headline, was the story of Chiang's takeover in Shanghai, there on the page to be seen if we had the eyes to see it. We most surely did look eagerly that morning to see what the paper had to say about the fire. But I could not remember being in the slightest degree aware of what was happening on the other side of the *Times'* front page. From this I draw my first lesson: if events are going to register on you in any way at all, *you have to be tuned in.* If for whatever reason you are not, events pass you by or, more important in the case of the historian, you pass them by.

Now when you do tune in—to go on to my second remark—you do

so on some particular wavelength. Let me illustrate again from this same experience. I had developed a strong interest in China before I finished my undergraduate terms at Columbia. It was nascently an interest in history and politics, and I devoured a small library of books on modern Chinese history, especially the history of China's experience with encroaching Western power during the preceding century. This interest was strong enough to cause me, as soon as I was free to move, to head for China to see it for myself. This was a move compounded of many things (for how many reasons might not a nineteen-year-old want to see what was on the far side of the world?), but in China my chief interest remained focussed on its current politics. In order to get a coherent view of what was happening there at the beginning of the 1930s, I quickly learned that I had to know more about the revolutionary events that had taken place during the 1920s and on back before that. This led me into a fresh and more intensive excursion into recent Chinese history. In all that I read during this time, I voraciously sought what we call facts, facts about the interplay of interests and nations, or classes and clashes, trade and the propagation of faiths, and—looking of course for the rights and wrongs of the human story—the sins of the strong and the sufferings of the weak. This is the stuff of history and politics and I took it all in in considerable amounts in as many different accounts and versions as I could find. Having developed some strong biases of my own, I had no difficulty instantly recognizing the biases of others. From this process of absorption-selection-acceptance-rejection I drew for myself a picture of one part of all this history—the Chinese revolution of 1925–27—and went on to add to the bibliographies a small historical work of my own about it.[1]

I mention all this because about twenty-five years later I went back to a great many of these same books, but this time I was seeking answers to an entirely different set of questions. How did the writer, I now wanted to know, *see* the Chinese, what kind of people did he make them appear to be, how did he feel about them? In many cases the copies of the books I re-read were off my own shelves, filled with the marginal notes, exclamations, and underlinings that marked my first reading. But now my pencil came down on entirely different passages, observations or remarks or judgments which my eye had slipped past quite heedlessly that long time before. I had learned early to be sensitive to bias—i.e. point of view—to know the meaning of the differences that emerged from reading, say, Carlyle or Kropotkin on the French Revolution, Trotsky or Carr on the Russian, Hua Kang or Tang Leang-li on the Chinese. But it had taken me a much longer time to become aware of the images held, by oneself and by others, as a key dimension of the perception of events and the people involved in them.

The study which had brought me to this experience was an examination of some of these images as they currently appeared in the minds of just under two-hundred American policy makers and opinion shapers, legislators, educators, editors, writers, churchmen, government officials—all individuals occupying key places in the communications network of the society. I set out to discover what they associated with China and the Chinese, with India and the Indians, to trace these associations in their minds back to their origins, and from there back into the mass media, the literature, the school texts, the history, to which they had been exposed. The results of this study appeared in 1958 in a book called *Scratches on Our Minds: American Images of China and India*.[2]

Among many other things, I found a close relationship between the sets of images these Americans had developed in their minds about the Chinese and the successive stages of power and powerlessness through which the Chinese had passed during the long period of contact between China and the United States. I also located the special source of some of the extraordinary and unique emotions felt by Americans in relation to China in the effect of the American missionary enterprise that for such a long time dominated the relationship and created the main channels of communication about it. The study of perceptions of India showed, again among many other things, that some kinds of cultural difference are just about unbridgeable. This work also showed how directly an individual's perceptions of another people and another culture are shaped and colored by his own particular window on the world: the time, place and circumstances of the encounter, his particular background and education, the elements of his own unique personality (an unseen specter hovering in, over, and behind all these responses), and the political conditions, the power relations, existing at the time when these ideas were fixed in his mind. Another thing it showed was that the best-schooled minds are embarrassingly capable of carrying the most flagrant prejudices and stereotypes, that these can be based on both ample and scanty experience, and that they can be held firmly over years, even a whole lifetime, without ever coming under critical examination.

These had often been acquired in early childhood, from listening to visiting missionaries, from putting coins in the collection to help the good work, from some single brush with a fellow traveler or a classmate, a brief experience, short journey, the impact of some event, or often from some single book. One individual who became a senior policy maker in the government had his highly favorable images of China and the Chinese fixed for life during a brief tour as a teacher in a mission school in China —the deferential behavior of the students had won him forever. Another, retired from a long career in government service connected to China, summoned up a nightmare he had experienced in his boyhood after reading a magazine story about cruelty inflicted on Christians in China during the Boxer Rebellion. No one seemed exempt from witlessly generalizing from tiny facts or fleeting experiences, or from clinging to fixed ideas, no matter how extended his contact with ever-changing, ever-varying actuality. This was especially true among individuals of a certain age who had read Pearl S. Buck's *The Good Earth,* probably in the China case the most influential single example of this kind of shaping influence.[3] Together with the film made from it, this book probably had more than anything else to do with shaping the images of China held by a whole generation of Americans, just as a few years earlier, on a somewhat less inclusive scale, Katherine Mayo's *Mother India* had done so much to reinforce and shape for its generation of readers certain popularly-held images of India.[4]

Another finding richly illustrated in this material was that these stereotypes and attitudes occur almost always in pairs, making up a crowded array of coupled pluses and minuses in the arks of our minds, counterparts of "good" and "bad," or "goodie-images" and "baddie-images," which can be summoned up or dismissed according to need. In most significant cases, this need is a political need. Thus Americans hold in their minds about the Chinese (and in a blurry "Oriental" way, for the Japanese as well) an assortment on the one hand of what I have called the Marco Polo-to-Pearl Buck images, and on the other the Genghis Khan–to-Fu Manchu images, the great "goodie" Chinese who were "wise" and the great "baddie" Chinese who were "fiendishly clever," the "thrifty" and the "miserly," the people with their great capacity for inflicting violence and cruelty. Such twin sets of qualities are handy things to have around in the press of conflict, for when events demand it, we need only push the right button and bring forth from our mental computers all the appropriate sets of images and their attached emotions. In almost every case, moreover, one can do this without being wholly false to the reality. The Chinese heroes of the 1940s became the Chinese monsters of the 1950s without having to move very far from the one compartment to the other in anyone's mind.

These sets of images are acquired over time and are communicated by a great variety of means, by travelers' accounts, by the gleanings that fall out over larger publics from the interests and works of traders, writers, scholars, artists, and in the case of China, especially the missionaries. The merchant mariners, like Franklin Roosevelt's grand-uncle Delano of New England who sailed the China coast, brought back wealth and crockery and romantic tales, and the Concordians who were interested in philosophy brought ideas about both Chinese and Hindu philosophies into the stream of American thought. The first important scholars in the field, like the historian Samuel Wells Williams, were missionaries, and the same tradition has been pursued into our own generation by others, like the historian Kenneth Latourette.[5] But to such sources over time we have to add all that gets communicated—increasingly in greater and greater volume—about events, contacts, contentions, collisions through the mass media, books, journals, newspapers, films, and radio and television, each bit becoming part of the process of creating and summoning up relevant images in people's minds, an item in the intimate interaction in the ways people perceive other people, how they interpret others' behavior, and how they behave themselves.

In the case of China it was possible to trace the acquistion and relevance of these paired views and paired attitudes through a long succession of historic periods, beginning with what I have called the Age of Respect when travelers and scholars of the Europe of Voltaire's time were filled with admiring wonder over the glories of Chinese civilization. Here we find not only attempts to borrow and apply Chinese political thought but also the vogue for chinoiseries in fashionable Europe, trinkets, toys, gadgets, and the building of a Chinese summer house in every nobleman's garden. Successful Western encroachment in the early nineteenth century brought on the discovery that the Chinese were weak and helpless, abruptly ushering in the Age of Contempt. By the end of that century the Chinese had been almost totally prostrated and their country brought to the edge of dismemberment, and the Boxer Rebellion, a last weak gasp of Chinese counter-assertion, was crushed. This led to the Age of Benevolence, a time when Western attitudes were dominated by more or less contemptuous patronage, and among Americans particularly, by an impressively self-righteous paternalism. Benevolence lasted for as long as Western white man walked as lord of all he surveyed in China. It was shaken by the abortive Chinese national revolutionary upheaval of the 1920s when the Chinese finally stood up by themselves to the latecoming Japanese would-be conquerors. The war was followed by the Communist conquest, carrying us into our present phase, a time of fearful respect or respectful fear, in which all these attitudes are blended in new ways and new combinations. It completes the circle in more ways than one, for it is not unreasonable to say, I suppose, that the clever Chinese never seemed more clever than in his seemingly successful thrust to revitalize old China, never so fearful and indifferent to individual humanity as in his total mobilization of the Chinese masses to this purpose, never more massively numerous, never more faceless, never more inscrutable than he has managed to appear in the latest phases of the so-called cultural revolution in Communist China.

Now each of these successive stages of experiences wove its own patterns of perception and image, each one reproduced and elaborated in every available form, carried along every channel of communication, appearing as fact or fiction, usually in the most vagrant bits and pieces and fleeting impressions marginal to the main business of every person's life. In this way they get imbedded in the minds of generations of people as each one is exposed to the reflections of these events and relationships in school textbooks, popular fiction, travelers' tales, at church, in newspapers and journals, and for the past half-century, in the most pervasively powerful of all media, the popular film, more recently multiplied in its spread and effect by its translation into television and radio, made nearly universal in its reach now by the transistor.

The sets of images created by this experience are formed for us in endlessly repeated cycles that give way to one another in response to the demand of events. To take only some of the recent examples of this process, perhaps some of you may be old enough to remember the rise of the fictional character of Fu Manchu in the 1920s, that superhumanly and fiendishly clever, fiendishly cruel and evil genius who served for a good many years as the quintessence of the Chinese negatively seen. He was the creature of an English writer known as Sax Rohmer but was the proto-type for a great mass of American Chinatown thrillers in magazine, cheap books, and in films. In the mid-1930s when Japan began its attacks on China and the Chinese gradually gathered themselves to offer resistance, and the American conscience was pricked by the plight of America's Chinese wards, the climate was cleared for the appearance of more favorable images of the Chinese. Not as responses to anybody's Machia-vellian (or Fu Manchu-ish) button-pushing, but nevertheless appearing in response to the need, came not only Pearl Buck's epochal image-changing and image-forming novel, but another fictional character whom you must certainly know, the Honolulu policeman Charlie Chan, who was not fiendishly clever but virtuously clever, not an evil genius but a "goodie" genius, popping up mysteriously from behind sliding panels, just as Fu Manchu and his minions used to do, but doing so now on the side of law and righteousness. His wisdom ("Confucius say") and unusual mental powers (the damned clever Chinese), and his mysteriousness and strangeness were all essentially the same qualities possessed by Fu Man-chu, but arrayed now with the angels. Charlie Chan ran his course through dozens of enormously popular films for about twenty years. The obvious postscript follows. In the mid-1950s there was an attempt at a full-scale revival of Fu Manchu, this time on television. Again, this was no deliberate political manipulation. A show-business agent in New York thought he had hit on a great idea since now the Chinese were villains again. The films were made and the show ran for a trial thirteen weeks. But it fell flat. The reality of fearful monsterhood represented by super-totalitarian China had hopelessly outstripped the pathetic little wickedness of Sax Rohmer's fictional criminal genius.

Consider at another level of this experience the over-idealization of Chinese heroism in the late 1930s and early 1940s and the transfer to the Japanese of all the evil, cruel, treacherous characteristics that had been attached for so long to the "baddie-images" of the Chinese. These were, I must remind you, not wispy myths or inventions. None of these images is ever wholly false any more than it is ever wholly true. Like heroism and sacrifice, cruelty and violence are surely a part of the Chinese reality, and there was nothing wispy or mythical about the Japanese army's rape of Nanking in 1937, or the Bataan Death March in 1942. With the war's end, however, and the Communist conquest of China, these Genghis Khan images were promptly restored to Mao Tse-tung and his cohorts. And now that the Japanese had so abruptly become our actual or prospective allies against the Mongol hordes of the mainland, the Japanese resumed the costume in which they had been shown to Americans long, long before, by Lafcadio Hearn and others, a small people of enormous vitality and delicate artistry, powerfully energetic and productive, and now once more, oh so attractive and admirable.

The point of all this, my third point—that you are tuned in—is you are tuned in on some particular wavelength, and *at some particular time.* History used to give us more time, longer intervals between the needs to shift our inter-national or inter-racial or inter-cultural focus, between these sets of images in our minds. There are one or two examples of remarkable persistence of the one set or the other. The common Western image of the terrible Turks, to name one, was held almost without contradiction from the time of the Crusades up into our own time. On the Bogardus Social Distance Scales, tested on American groups first in 1928, the Turk showed up more or less consistently at the bottom of every category, along with and often lower even than the Jews and the Negroes.[6] It was not until the Korean War that an allied Turkish brigade fighting alongside Americans and South Koreans introduced, almost for the first time in American minds, a favorable image of Turks. But note well that this switch took place, as so often happens, around the same characteristic that had been most prominently attached to its negative counterpart. Turkish ferocity—nourished by fact and lore from the days of the Saracens to the massacres of the Armenians—on the battlefields of Korea became the admirable bravery of doughty warriors. In more recent times the scenes have shifted on us much more rapidly. I am sure other examples will occur to you out of our recent experiences: the need to keep our images in line with our shifting alliances and allegiances in world politics—in relation, for example, to the Germans and the Russians—have put us all on a kind of flying trapeze swinging in great and dizzying whooshes across the arenas of our contemporary history.

It is crucial to remember, however, that these paired sets of images, created by long historic experience and planted in our minds generation after generation by this process of programming, *all* persist throughout the whole period of time. They move in and out of people's minds, never wholly displacing each other, always coexisting, each ready to respond to the call of fresh circumstances, always new, yet instantly garbed in all the words and pictures of a rich lore, made substantial and unique in each historic experience by the reality of recurring experience. People enter and exit from this process at different times, the demands shift at differing rates, and under different pressures. In the panel of Americans I interviewed for a study I made in the 1950s, I found individuals whose governing notions about China located them at every point in this long continuum, each one making the necessary transition or adjustment needed to fit his attitudes to the new actualities. There were those who still thought of the Chinese as contemptible weaklings subject to power and authority in the blindest kind of submissive way, and who therefore saw the Communist victory as the latest demonstration of the sheeplike qualities of the Chinese masses. There were also those who held the Chinese in the most uncritically benevolent admiration, and therefore often tended to argue (how odd it sounds now!) that the Communist revolution was really not "Chinese" at all, but "Russian." Those—and there were many—who held in their minds the fearful images of the cruel and dangerous and devious Chinese found that their feelings had been powerfully reactivated and reinforced by the Communist conquest of power.

I began by suggesting that historians and social scientists, indeed all who write, are people too, and subject to this same array of experiences and exposures, and accustomed to forming many of their mental holdings in the same unthinking way. I can give you the example—not an isolated one—of a nationally known writer who, when asked what came to his mind about Indians, came up instantly with the memory of a fellow student he had known when he was a Rhodes scholar at Oxford thirty years before, a Sikh who had lived in his house and was "the only man there who left hairs in the bathtub." Announcing this, his voice took on the same rasp of disgusted annoyance it must have had on mornings way back then when he confronted that unsightly tub. From this—he had no occasion in his life to concern himself with India or Indians—he had erected a whole set of notions about Indians. They were sloppy, he told me, careless of the needs of others, egocentric, and unpleasant.

Historians, social scientists, intellectuals generally, I have suggested, also have to be tuned in, and tuned in on certain wavelengths and at particular times. Hence the content and caliber of much of their work. Consider what our history and geography textbooks in this society contained, say about Asia—about China, Japan, India—until the day before yesterday. In 1944 a study of American textbooks in most common use in elementary and secondary schools showed that only seven percent of the space of the geography texts was devoted to Asia, and in world history textbooks, "not more than 1% is devoted to the rise and development of national cultures of this part of the world where half of the world's population lives." Another study of twenty-six world history texts and eighteen geography texts published between 1902 and 1917—that was when my generation went to elementary school—found that from one to one-and-a-half percent of the space was given over to China in some of the books, while others omitted it entirely. A 1939 study showed three percent of world history texts devoted to China and Japan. In a 1959 study of twenty-eight world history and twenty-seven geography texts—the most widely used in the country—it was shown that one-and-a-half percent of the history text space and two-and-a-half percent of the geography text space were allotted to India.[7] If you consider how important, even how critical these areas of the world have come to be for us in these past few years, you can appreciate why we are now in a desperate scramble to produce new and somewhat better-balanced textbooks that take Asia's existence into larger account.

Take another even more pressing immediate example. What do you suppose a detailed study would show, not only in textbooks but in all the works of history and so-called social studies, about the place of the Negro in American society from the beginning up to the day before yesterday? With virtually no exceptions, works of this kind produced by white scholars reflected the dominant outlooks and attitudes concerning Negroes over these generations. Why do you suppose John Hope Franklin and whole committees of suddenly-galvanized teachers and scholars now have to produce new works which will begin to include material no one thought was important before but which has suddenly become critically important, a matter of utmost national concern? It was only the Negro historians, beginning in the last century with George Washington Williams and going on through to Rayford W. Logan and John Hope Franklin, who tried to bring the position of Negroes into the larger picture.[8] Long ago Logan was looking into the public prints and popular arts of the closing decades of the last century to show how the Negro had reached the nadir of his position as the bottom-most member of the American society. It has taken years and decades and rather pressing changes, events, crises, to bring others to see—not only white people but white historians too—what has been outside that window in full view all the time.

So now, one may ask, what materials are historians to use to do better than they have? Someone in this group this morning spoke of the scholar in 1984 looking back on this period and wondering how to put it together coherently. Paul Lazarsfeld was probably right in saying that he would have so much material that he will choke on it. But have no fear. He will have his biases, his blind spots, his special interests; he will have *his* view of what lies outside that window. And I have no doubt that he will be able to select whatever he feels he needs to write his history of our time. But the effort to see beyond these limits has become part of the scholar's programming. We do already have a good body of work by individuals who are trying to add these more varied insights to their rendering of events past. Philip Curtin's *The Image of Africa* is an unusually striking example of a historian's effort to discover why and how people developed the sets of mind which led them to shape the policies they pursued, in this case toward the slave trade or the problems of how to settle in and organize Africa.[9] This is going to be harder to do about the past than about the present. But there must be mountains of material that historians have never thought to tap if only because they never dreamed that it was relevant to anything they thought was important.

There is a final remark I would like to add here on a matter that has flickered in and out of this discussion. This is the question of how much we can know or say about how far these images, these predispositions, these pictures in our heads, *do* figure in the making of actual policy decisions. This is more than asking how public opinion affects such decisions. It is a further step removed. Katz and Lazarsfeld's landmark analysis of the two-step system of communication showed us a model of how much of our information is sifted through influentials of various kinds to the masses beyond. But my question has to do with what the influentials have in their heads to begin with. If we carry this over to the field of policy, it is obvious that there is much we might still learn.

Think of some of the key men who have been concerned with the making of our history, especially, say, in relation to China, or Africa. Among the chief policy makers from Elihu Root to John Foster Dulles, and on down to Dean Rusk and Lyndon B. Johnson, I am certain that a million subjects still await their authors. Let me cite one example: Howard K. Beale's examination of Theodore Roosevelt's policy behavior toward China shortly after the turn of this century. Roosevelt was the product of his time; he had a strong view of the Chinese as contemptible weaklings with whom there was no point in trying to deal except by force. Thus, when the declining Chinese dynasty began to give way to reform and there was a chance for American interests to ally themselves with the reform movement, Roosevelt was not interested. When in 1905 the Chinese staged their first anti-foreign boycott, directed against Americans in protest against the maltreatment of Chinese in the United States, Roosevelt was prepared to send in the navy and the marines to end the nonsense. Beale examined Roosevelt's notions about the Chinese and concluded: "The block to Roosevelt's understanding was the inability he shared with many Americans of his day to associate qualities and aspiration of 'superior people' with the Chinese. His persistence in regarding them, because of military weakness and industrial underdevelopment, as 'a backward people' destroyed the effectiveness of his policy in the Far East." From this Beale went on to attribute to this failing of the first Roosevelt all the failures of American policy in China ever since.[10]

It is a virgin field. Take Woodrow Wilson's ability to compromise with the Japanese at Versailles on the subject of Shantung. He was ready to "give" Shantung to the Japanese, a shocking betrayal of China's dearest nationalist hopes, in return for Japan's acceptance of his fourteen points. It was also in return for some relaxation of Japanese pressure on American racist practices as they affected the Japanese in the United States. What were Wilson's pictures-in-the-head about the Chinese? About the Japanese? What was able to cut across his political professions about self-determination and his moral professions about the dignity of man? It would be worth someone's time to find out.

Or think a moment of Roosevelt II. Franklin D. Roosevelt never tired, whenever the question of China came up, of telling visitors about his grand-uncle Delano who engaged in the opium trade off the China coast.[11] Franklin grew up in an environment full of the mental and physical bric-a-brac that related to China in the nineteenth century, the time of the freebooting imperialists, their imposed "unequal treaties," their contempt for the right or ability of the Chinese to serve their own interests. It cannot be wholly far-fetched to imagine a linkage between these exposures and the ability of F. D. Roosevelt, the great democrat and libertarian, to strike a deal with Stalin at Yalta in 1945 at China's expense in the best freebooting imperialist manner of 1898. The Chinese were not even present at the conference, but Roosevelt felt quite able to assure his post-Czarist super-imperialist Russian host that the Chinese would be brought to the heel of the conditions fixed without their own consent at Yalta.

Along such lines much work waits to be done by historians. The application of fresh insights to history and the behavior of historic individuals is only just beginning. Historians are beginning to be jostled by other students of society and by students of culture and personality, and of the individual psyche. Very little of this is likely to profit from the more quantified and computerising social science techniques, but all of it will certainly profit from the great variety of new ways of looking at the human story which are coming into view as the old intellectual crusts break open. The work I am speaking for here will still be much more a work of art than of science, but art more closely and more intimately linked to more dimensions of the reality, a greater art, in short, than most historians have managed to achieve in their work up to now.

Comment 4

◆

Athan Theoharis

DEPARTMENT OF HISTORY, MARQUETTE UNIVERSITY

ADDRESSING THE QUESTION of the "Sources for Images of Foreign Countries," Isaacs has presented a lively and suggestive paper which, however, suffers from a certain vagueness and confusion of focus. His account, relying on his excellent *Scratches on Our Minds* as well as wide and varied personal experiences, is at best an introduction to research problems and at worst an example of the need for more rigorous scholarship and a stricter concern for methodology.

At the outset I must agree with Isaacs' contention that the historian and social scientist, as well as the policy maker and general public, have subjective biases and perceptions that influence their images of foreign countries. That they operate on particular wavelengths cannot be doubted. What Isaacs might profitably have explored in greater depth are the factors that influence particular perceptions and contribute to changing images, and the extent to which images influence policy formation and public opinion. Indeed, "pictures in the head" might or might not be important in the formulation of policy or the development of public opinion. The prevalence of particular images, their relevance and impact, must be ascertained through empirical means, such as content analysis or the sophisticated public opinion poll. The relationship between image and public opinion and image and policy formation must be confirmed, not implied.

Moreover, Isaacs presents certain impressions and experiences as examples of sources; he neither explores the representative character of nor the alternative explanations and questions raised by these examples. Thus, he relates the interesting story of the former Oxonian whose view of India allegedly was shaped by his unpleasant association with a Sikh. In like manner, he asserts that "one individual who became a senior policy maker in the government had his highly favorable images of China *fixed for life* during a brief tour as a teacher in a mission school in China" (italics mine). Similarly, he emphasizes the impact of Fu Manchu and Pearl Buck's *Good Earth* on public images of China. Finally, he argues that stereotypes and attitudes "almost always" come in good-evil pairs. But all of this, while charming and more or less acceptable, is not very useful for the historian. We must be able to confirm impact and influence; to document, for example, who and how significant a sector of American society read *The Good Earth* and how their image of China was shaped by this classic. These research problems, however, are simple in comparison with the difficulty of ascertaining the complex, confusing, and contradictory character of the image of China elicited by the reading of this book in the thirties.

In addition, Isaacs' impressionistic approach leads him to ignore other variables that contribute to the development of image. His example of the shifting positive and negative images of Turkey provides a case in point. Isaacs observes that the persistence of the image of the ferocious Turk resulted, paradoxically, in an unfavorable view of Turkey in 1928 and a favorable one in 1950. But he failed to explore the possible importance of the climate of these specific periods, specifically the radically different values and priorities in 1928 and 1950. In 1950 policy was based on strength (NATO) and in 1928 on essentially pacifistic, nonmilitary grounds (Kellogg-Briand pact). Isaacs' Turkish example raises two possible concerns for the historian: first, how important was the specific time or policy context to image formation; and second, how important were the dominant values and traditions of the general society?

Images, as well as policy and opinion, are derived from a welter of factors whose origins are not readily ascertained. Isaacs' analysis focuses on the importance of personal or childhood experiences. He does not assess the possible importance of transitory strategic considerations and the role of policy makers in the formation of public opinion. In reviewing Isaacs' assertion that the the two Roosevelts' negative image of China shaped their China policy, I would question whether these images had been fixed in childhood or whether images as opposed to power realities were the factors that ultimately shaped their policy responses. To rephrase Isaacs, was Theodore Roosevelt's China policy based on his view of the weak Chinese or on Far Eastern power realities? Was Franklin Roosevelt's Yalta policy based on impressions about China derived from familial ties or on the military and political situation in 1945? Were the two Roosevelts influenced significantly, peripherally, or not at all by images of earlier experiences? The degree of childhood or perception influence on the policy maker deserves exploration; it has real relevance for the diplomatic historian. But merely asserting this and developing a workable methodology are two different things.

Because he focuses primarily on elite opinion and the policy implications of image, Isaacs also fails to discuss the principal subject before us—how to determine public opinion and its impact on policy decisions. Two questions require some consideration. First, does public image shape or is it shaped by policy? Second, what insights can the diplomatic historian gain by exploring the sources for images? I intend to explore briefly a single but nonetheless important research problem.

Invariably, the diplomatic historian confronts a striking disparity between an administration's rhetoric and its substantive actions and concerns. If policy is generally presented in idealistic and democratic terms, its effect might contradict those stated aims. Is there, then, a distinctly different image held by elites and by the public? To what extent do policy decisions and rhetoric influence public images? Were public images of China, Germany, Japan, or the Soviet Union significantly influenced by experience, policy, or rhetoric, or more likely, by what blend of the three? Each of these facets requires intensive analysis.

In addition, the prevalence of mythical beliefs must be explored in assessing the distinction between policy rationale and result. Thus, is rhetoric simply a subterfuge, is it uncritically believed by both policy maker and public, or does it, by influencing perception and policy priorities, eventually come to be believed? To use one of Isaacs' examples: what factors contributed to the shift in public images of China and Japan in the 1940s? Why did the positive qualities of the China image outweigh the negative ones during one period and not another, and why the reverse of this process for Japan?

In concluding, I would not discount the relevance of a study of the sources for images of foreign countries. In his paper Isaacs provides many valuable suggestions for the historian. My main criticism of the paper is methodological: Isaacs' failure to document or critically assess the factors contributing to image formation and the nature of the relationship of image to policy making and public opinion.

A study of the sources for images is essential for the historian of both public opinion and policy formation. Policy is not made in a vacuum, either on the domestic, the personal, or the international scene. Just as the policy maker's responses are limited by existing options and realities, so too do the policy maker's and the general public's perceptions and fears establish other, real limits. The factors that serve to develop particular perceptions, and the durability and importance of these perceptions, require as extensive an examination by the historian as the heretofore limited diplomatic research centering on treaties, wars, and alliances. The sources for that research are legion, as they include personal diaries and memoirs, recorded experiences, travelogs, popular novels, movies, textbooks, letters and other forms of correspondence. The parochial diplomatic historian must move beyond the traditional bounds of his discipline and acquire an understanding of not only international and political developments but also the cultural and intellectual history of the United States. The "Sources for Images of Foreign Countries" constitutes one part of that challenge for the diplomatic historian.

Part Three
METHOD

5

Undoubtedly, images of foreign countries are purveyed in an almost infinite variety of sources from grammar school lessons to chance meetings with hyphenate-Americans. If the problems involved in defining or delimiting sources are difficult ones, those relating to analysis and interpretation are even more so. Traditionally, historians studying image or opinion have read deeply in what they considered to be a representative sample in an attempt to discern patterns or themes. Employing their training, intelligence, and judgment, they emerge from this heady immersion in source materials and present their findings. The results of this process are seen today in their most sophisticated form in the American Studies movement. While scholars in this area have contributed significantly to our understanding of American values and images, they have devoted little time to the explanation of their method.

Of course, to explain the methodology of American Studies or intellectual history is like attempting to nail the proverbial jelly to the wall, but here Leo Marx takes up the challenge. His The Machine in the Garden (1964) *represents well the approach of his discipline.*

Edward Lurie, who evaluates Marx's article, is the author of Louis Agassiz: A Life in Science (1960), *and a student of American intellectual history. Lurie has also directed and taught in the American Studies program at Wayne State University.*

American Studies:
A Defense of an Unscientific Method

◆

Leo Marx

DEPARTMENT OF ENGLISH, AMHERST COLLEGE

THE LETTER INVITING me to join this symposium is a triumph of tact. It asks me to represent my colleagues, certain literary critics and cultural historians associated with the American Studies movement, and to describe and defend our "methodology."[1] Our courteous host, pretending to be unaware of the widely accepted view that American Studies does not in fact possess a method, implies that we must have been too busy to put it in writing. "Nowhere," he says, "does the historian have an outline of this important approach to the study of images and symbols." The flattering implication is that once our procedure is systematized and made available it will be useful to historians, including those who consider themselves social scientists, and perhaps even the most rigorous empiricists who specialize in the study of public opinion. Such at least is the promise held forth by the present meeting. Let me say at once that I am skeptical but willing to try. My feeling, to borrow some phrases used by Ezra Pound on another subject, is that the schools of scholarship represented here have detested one another long enough. Who knows? We might have something to teach each other: let there be commerce between us.

But in what sense can American Studies be said to have a method? The authoritative answer to that question was given in 1957 by Henry Nash Smith. In his essay "Can 'American Studies' Develop a Method?" Smith not only acknowledged our notorious methodological deficiencies, but he concluded his judicious observations by asserting that nothing like a codifiable, overall method for American Studies was in sight.[2] (Ten years have passed, it is true, but there is no reason to think that today

Smith would need to change that assertion in any significant way.) At first his seemingly pessimistic conclusion dismayed a number of his colleagues, but eventually many, perhaps most, have come around to his point of view, and now some of us are prepared to carry his argument even further. So far, that is, as the tacit definition of what constitutes an acceptable scholarly method is borrowed, by whatever circuitous route, from the physical sciences, then I for one would argue that it is neither possible nor desirable for American Studies to develop a method.[3]

To say this, however, is not to admit that our work is merely capricious or impressionistic. My purpose in what follows, therefore, is to be as explicit as possible in describing our assumptions and procedures. If they embody the rudiments of a method, it is one that admittedly invites the epithet *unscientific*. A less invidious term, however, would be *humanistic*. To clarify the distinction, which turns upon the vital relation between statements of fact and judgments of value, I shall begin with a contrast between two ways of studying group consciousness: that of the empirical historian (or sociologist) who is a practitioner of content analysis, and that of the humanistic scholar working in American Studies. Each is engaged in an essentially historical enterprise: the effort to describe and understand the state of mind of a group (or groups) of people at some moment in the past. Yet each would consider the work of the other inadequate and probably misleading. The comparison is a nice example of the difference between the social scientific and humanistic disciplines, a difference that is in many ways less obvious, and more difficult to clarify, than that between the physical sciences and the humanities. Let me begin by comparing the aims of the two schools, the criteria according to which they select their materials, and their respective methods of analysis. I shall then try to indicate certain ways in which the methods are in fact complementary. For this purpose I propose to describe, in some detail, an example of the procedures used in American Studies.

1. *The Methods of "Content Analysis" and "American Studies" Compared.* What are the aims of each method? In large measure the aims of content analysis are determined and limited by an *a priori* methodological commitment. As Harold Lasswell and his colleagues put it some twenty years ago, content analysis is "a technique which aims at optimum objectivity, precision, and generality in the analysis of symbolic behavior;

its value is to be appraised according to the success with which it achieves these aims in specific researches."[4] In practice, and judging by the current work of such content analysts as Richard L. Merritt, this means that the method is limited to problems susceptible to "the systematic tabulation of the frequency with which certain predetermined symbols or other variables appear in a given body of data."[5] For the content analyzer, in short, the goal of any specific inquiry must be compatible with a prior methodological restriction: the insistence upon obtaining quantifiable results.

For the humanist working in American Studies, on the other hand, considerations of method are secondary. He defines his purpose without reference to any methodological restrictions, but rather in relation to a vast, apparently limitless subject matter. According to Smith, the aim of American Studies is "the investigation of American culture, past and present, as a whole."[6] The phrase "as a whole" is the key to many of the distinctive features of this interdisciplinary approach; in practice, Smith explains, it does not signal an attempt to deal indiscriminately with all kinds of behavior, but rather to select topics which involve decisive relationships.[7] Much of the interesting work in American Studies has concentrated upon points of intersection between existential reality, the collective consciousness, and individual products of mind; or to use a simpler language, between historical fact, culture, and particular works. (They may be works of art, music, engineering, political theory, philosophy, literature—in other words, any creations of man.) Thus the specific problem with which I have been concerned, and which I propose to discuss in some detail, is the interplay, in the period before the Civil War, between industrialization, the prevailing attitudes of the American people, and the work of certain major writers, Henry Thoreau and Herman Melville, for example. My purpose has been to discover the most significant relationships among these phenomena, to learn how they illuminate each other, and to see whether such an interdisciplinary approach to the culture "as a whole" provides insights not otherwise obtainable. The subject clearly does not lend itself to quantification or optimum objectivity. Although the content analyzer and the humanist share a general aim —the interpretation of symbolic behavior—they define their specific objectives in wholly different ways.

A marked difference also is evident in the criteria that each invokes in selecting materials for study. Given his prior commitment to system-

atic, objective, replicatible research, the empirical scholar who selects a
problem susceptible to content analysis either must study all the relevant
data or make a selection in accordance with the principles of scientific
sampling. The significant point, so far as the contrast with the humanistic
method is concerned, is that the empiricist may *not* invoke qualitative
standards of selection. This restriction would seem to make it difficult, if
not impossible, to give any special attention to major works of art or
philosophy or other products of the "high" culture. How, for example,
does the content analyst choose works of imaginative literature for the
study of American attitudes toward industrialization before the Civil
War? Since it hardly is possible for him to read all the writing of the
period, and since it would be misleading (even if it were possible) to
single out works which are in some immediately manifest sense "about"
industrialization (the most complex and perceptive responses often were
oblique or covert, hence not readily identifiable), the content analyzer
must rely upon an arbitrary or random sampling procedure. It is almost
certain, therefore, that his sample will not include either Thoreau's *Walden* or Melville's *Moby Dick*.

The exponent of content analysis, it should be said, might meet this
objection in several ways. He might exclude all imaginative literature
from his sample on the ground that it seldom exercises a significant
influence upon public opinion. Or he might take the best-seller list (or
some other measure of contemporary popularity) as the basis for his
selection of imaginative literature. To be sure, this criterion also would
exclude the two masterpieces mentioned, but then we must acknowledge
that even a sample of books influential with the elite audience of the
period would not include them. When first published they had few
readers and virtually no influence. Nevertheless, let us suppose that the
content analyzer wants to include a sample of the "high" culture in his
survey of American responses to industrialization between 1830 and 1860.
One obvious procedure would be for him to select a body of current
opinion—current, that is, in the 1960s—as the basis for his choice. He
might select the works to be analyzed from the reading lists of college
courses in American literature, or from the most widely used anthologies,
or from critical articles in literary journals. After all, the "high" culture of
the past has been defined retrospectively. And though the resulting
sample would of course be based upon a value judgment, it would be an

impersonal, collective judgment, a consensus of informed opinion rather than an individual preference. The really difficult problem the content analyst faces in dealing with imaginative literature is not the selection but the interpretation of the material.

Turning now to the criteria the humanist invokes in choosing his subject matter, given his aim—the study of the culture as a whole—it is evident that he must have in view an abstract model, however crude, from which to derive the categories for classifying his materials. One obvious shortcoming of the American Studies movement has been a reluctance to make explicit such models or working assumptions. In the case at hand, for example, I have taken industrialization as an historical starting point or primary "event"; it signifies a vital change in the conditions of life in America at the time, a change that can be located in the category of knowledge closest to existential reality, or what Hannah Arendt has called "factual truth": that "brutally elementary data . . . whose indestructibility has been taken for granted even by the most extreme and most sophisticated believers in historicism."[8] (In the present example, economic statistics provide a rough measure of the rate of industrialization, and we have fairly reliable data on the introduction of various kinds of power machinery, urbanization, etc.) On this model the contents of the culture belong to a higher level of abstraction. The culture may be defined as a system, or interrelated group of systems, of values, meanings, and goals. Regional, class, or ethnic subcultures, as well as the literary "high" culture, must be included among the systems embraced by the national culture. The identification of these subcultures also requires a concept of the social structure—a point we shall return to. In distinguishing the two methods, however, the significant point is the indispensability to the humanist, and in spite of its ambiguous sociological status, of the category of "high" culture. Any set of criteria which did not enable him to select major works of thought and expression would be wholly unacceptable.

The judgment implicit in the concept of "high" culture marks a crucial distinction between the methods of the humanist and the social scientist. To invoke it is admittedly to employ a value judgment in the selection of data; but then, of course, all students of the humanities rely, to a degree seldom acknowledged, upon the judgment of others in selecting their subject matter. Consider the scholar who is regarded as an "expert" in American literature. In fact he is expert about a relatively small fraction of the whole body of American writing. Those works have been sifted out by an endless, collective process of evaluation. To be sure, he may have made his own sample of popular and now largely forgotten works, but he cannot be said to "know" American writing in the sense of having made an independent selection of the most significant works from that immense collection of printed matter. His inquiry necessarily begins, therefore, with the established canon—a selection, we trust, based on the collective wisdom, which presumably includes the most fully realized, complex and powerful (hence enduring) work of American writers.[9] Because this canon presumably embodies the highest development of literary consciousness, it is a major source for the humanist in his continuing effort to recover the usable past. What requires emphasis here is the inherently, inescapably normative character of the intricate, never ending, and imperfectly understood process which brings the subject matter of the humanities into existence.

Let me compare, finally, the modes of analysis used by each school. It is evident that two basic assumptions distinguish the procedures of the empirical historian from those of the humanist. The first and more obvious follows directly from the former's insistence upon quantifiable results. Given this requirement, he must begin by formulating his problem in such a way that it can be solved, in the words of one exponent of content analysis, "by counting the appearance of a limited number of content variables in a given body of data." The second assumption is that the paraphrasable "message," either manifest or latent, is the truly significant feature of every verbal construct. Most of the procedures of content analysis rest upon these assumptions. It is a method, accordingly, that "focuses on the message, or the WHAT . . . It is the systematic, objective, and quantitative characterization of content variables manifest or latent in a message."[10]

The mode of analysis practiced by the humanistic scholar in American Studies is based upon quite different assumptions. For one thing, he assumes that the significant relationships cannot be reduced to quantifiable terms. The chasm between the two schools on this score is implicit in the quite different objects of their concern, to the difference, that is, between "culture" and "public opinion." But if the humanist cannot quantify his results, how does he meet the charge that they cannot be validated? How does he answer the empirical social scientist who says that what the humanist claims to be knowledge is indistinguishable from subjective opinion? Leaving aside the large and complicated problem of documentation or evidence in the humanities, the fact remains that here again the humanist relies, at bottom, upon the eventual achievement of a reliable scholarly consensus. He places his faith in the impersonal process of critical scholarship, trusting that in the long run it will correct or eliminate invalid observations, and that it will incorporate valid insights into the living body of knowledge.

Nor can the cultural historian go along with the content analyzer's second basic assumption, his almost exclusive emphasis upon the paraphrasable message. In analyzing verbal constructs the humanist may be as concerned with the HOW as the WHAT. At the outset, indeed, he postulates a distinction between the discursive and figurative uses of language, and although he cannot wholly separate them, in their purest embodiments he regards them as virtually distinct modes of discourse, one verging toward abstract logic, the other toward lyric poetry. Because the language of imaginative literature tends to be figurative, and because the controlling context of the individual work usually is imagistic or metaphoric, the message—the element reducible to a discursive statement—is only a part and not necessarily the most important part of the meaning. A large part of the meaning, in other words, resides in the inherent emotional power of the work. To fully apprehend the "content" of a novel or poem, therefore, it is necessary to get at those feelings, to sort them out, to name them, and to make their function explicit. For this purpose the student of literature has available the remarkably sensitive techniques of modern textual criticism. They enable him to understand the use of various literary devices to generate emotion. I am thinking of certain narrative methods in the novel, and their ironic implications, and of the subtle ways in which the explicit theme or "message" may be undercut, in poetry, by rhythm and tone; I am thinking, also, of the immense efficacy of the tacit, that is, of connotative figurative devices and imagery. But this is not the place to describe contemporary methods of literary analysis. Suffice it to say that they help to illuminate aspects of imaginative writing which are essential to its proper understanding but inaccessible to the reductive methods of the content analyzer.

So much, then, for the contrast between the two methods. It is clear that each is designed to provide different yet to some extent complementary kinds of knowledge. Content analysis enables the social scientist to reconstruct a pattern of group opinion as it existed at a particular time, unmodified by any external or retrospective observer's judgment of value. In order to gain such precise, objective knowledge, the practitioner of content analysis in effect excludes certain kinds of evidence. In theory, to be sure, the technique may be applied to any written work, but in practice it is useful chiefly for the analysis of material whose meaning is readily translated into a discursive statement. This means that content analysis is virtually useless in getting at the significance of imaginative writing. To the scholar working in American Studies, of course, this is a serious defect in the method; for him a description of the national consciousness which does not take literature into account is wholly inadequate. At bottom, no doubt, the difference comes down to opposed conceptions of what matters in the record of the past, indeed, to opposed definitions of historical reality. It is a difference implicit, to repeat, in the concepts "culture" and "public opinion." And yet it would be wrong to conclude that we are dealing with the familiar contrast between the literary and the social scientific mentalities, which is to say, between a concern with art and a concern with society. For if the American Studies movement has a distinctive goal, it is to cross that conventional academic barrier and to establish meaningful connections between the two kinds of knowledge. That is why the two methods may be regarded as complementary. By way of illustration, I shall now describe in some detail a sample inquiry in American Studies.

2. *A Sample Problem in American Studies.* The subject had caught my attention when I read a distinguished critic's remark to the effect that American writers had begun to manifest an awareness of industrialization between 1880 and 1900.[11] Intellectual and literary historians tended to accept this view, but it seemed to me wrong—or at least in need of serious qualification. I had recently been immersed in the work of writers who came to maturity in the 1830s, and it impressed me as deeply informed by the concerns we associate with industrialization. Writers like Emerson, Thoreau, Hawthorne, and Melville did not, to be sure, use the word itself, nor did they often write "about" the subject in the literal sense of describing social and economic change. But, like their European contemporaries, they were preoccupied with the theme of alienation—man's

alienation from both nature and himself—and much of their thinking turned upon the contrast between the artificial and the natural, the urban and the rural, and the paradox of simultaneously increasing collective power and individual powerlessness. To identify these themes was simple enough, but to relate them to an awareness of industrialization was not. In theory, then, the problem was to trace the impact upon consciousness of a change in existential reality *before* that change had been fully conceptualized. In this case the most tangible evidence was the striking prominence given by the writers mentioned to images drawn from the latest industrial technology. This fact in turn gave rise to certain obvious questions. How was this body of imagery related to the themes of the particular works in which it appeared? What were the connections between such relatively sophisticated writing, the dominant culture, and the demonstrable fact of industrialization?

The choice of literary material for this study presented no particular difficulty. It was based, as I have said, upon an initial familiarity with the major writers of the period. (Their status as "major," which is to say, their place in the "high" culture, had of course been determined for me by the conventional literary wisdom.) The first step, accordingly, was to read their work closely, in its entirety, and with special attention to the links between technological imagery and cardinal themes. The aim at this stage was to locate recurrent patterns of meaning. One observation that later proved to be of value was the simple fact that machine images seemed to take on symbolic power to the degree that they were coupled with images of landscape. What struck the literary imagination, in other words, was the symbolic contrast between the new industrial technology and the natural setting, either wild or rural. The terms *image* and *symbol,* as used in American Studies, derive from literary criticism, and while no absolutely precise distinction can be drawn between them, an *image* refers to a verbal recording of a simple sense perception, and it becomes a *symbol* to the degree that it is made to carry a burden of implication (value, association, feeling, or in a word, meaning) beyond that which is required for a mere reference.

The selection of materials from the general culture to represent what used to be called "the spirit of the age" was based upon more ambiguous principles. Moving out from the work of major writers, I read the work of men with lesser reputations, some of the popular or even subliterature of the period, and I examined magazines, newspapers, speeches, songs, diaries, and the graphic arts. At first the method was to read widely and at random in order to get an impression of the incidence and character of reactions to industrialization. Later I selected a few periodicals for a more extensive and somewhat more systematic study. In choosing them I was guided chiefly by the presence of relevant materials, and by the sociological identity or special bias of certain journals. From the vantage of the empirical social scientist this no doubt will seem one of the weakest features of the procedure, but there does not seem to be any obvious solution to the root problem here. The scholar wants to define certain pervasive attitudes in the culture, yet he knows that most of his sources represent the special interest of an economic class, or of a particular regional, political, religious, ethnic or vocational group. His only recourse, under the circumstances, is to take these biases into account, and to select sources which roughly approximate a cross-section of the national culture. To do this, of course, he must have some sort of sociological model in view, and for that he inevitably relies upon the general historian.[12] The procedure, in short, is to read the current historical literature, form a conception of the social structure, and use it as a frame for the evidence.

In selecting material from the journals singled out for relatively extensive study, the procedure was an informal version of the random sample. Depending upon the apparent density of the evidence, I might decide to read one issue of a monthly magazine for each year—a different month, of course—over a span of thirty years. If that sample did not seem adequate, the process was repeated. The test of an adequate sample was the yield of new evidence. When no new kinds of evidence were forthcoming, that is, when it seemed virtually certain that the next technological image would conform to one or another of a limited number of established patterns, the source was considered exhausted. At the more popular level the material fell more neatly into stereotypical categories. In any case, the nearest equivalent to validation here was the more or less predictable recurrence of certain patterns.

In this kind of inquiry the most interesting problems arise in establishing connections between particular works and the general culture. As all students of literature know, the relationship is always indirect, always modified by the interior history of literature itself. Let me illustrate with a specific example. My initial aim had been to discover responses to industrialization, and in the serious writing of the period I had found a recurrent use of the contrast between the machine and the natural landscape. In attempting to understand how this device comported with the larger design of the works in question, however, I came to realize that I was dealing with a modern, post-romantic, and in some respects peculiarly American version of an ancient literary mode—the pastoral. Before proceeding, therefore, it was necessary to shift attention from the interplay between literature and the extra-literary experience of the age to the relation between American writers of the period and their literary forbears. In other words, it was necessary to be clear about the pastoral mode, its origin and development, and the similarities and differences between American and earlier versions of pastoral.

To establish a degree of continuity between Thoreau and Shakespeare and Virgil was to recognize the evolution of literature—the interior development of its forms and conventions—as a semi-autonomous feature of the culture. This is only to say that in addition to his unique experience of his own age, each writer was influenced by writers who preceded him, particularly those whose work he in some sense emulated. When the cultural historian deals with a work of physics, sociology, or music, he confronts a similar point of intersection between the interior development of an intellectual discipline and an individual's special experience. Obvious though it is, the point often is neglected, and it complicates the procedures of content analysis in ways that are seldom discussed. (How, for example, does the analyst distinguish between the conventional element in a work and a response to the immediate environment?) In the specific inquiry being described, many of the literary works which embodied a significant response to industrialization proved to be pastorals. But although they were similar in many respects to traditional versions of pastoral, they also displayed marked differences which could be attributed, it seemed, to the special conditions of life in America. If there is a generalization about method to be made here, it is this: the conventional features of a work must be acknowledged and understood before the cultural historian can answer such important questions as: What made the convention relevant at the time? What modifications did the age make in the convention? How can the modifications be explained?

As a way of answering these questions, I sought and found a comparable pattern in the general culture. Here too, when technological images acquired a distinct symbolic power, they tended to be juxtaposed to images of landscape. Certain traditional features of literary pastoralism also were present. The contrast between the new machine power and the native landscape served to epitomize a contrast between two styles of life, one relatively complex and sophisticated, the other simple, contemplative, and dedicated to the pursuit of happiness. In the American imagination, that is, the conventional retreat of the shepherd or other pastoral figure from the corrupt world to the green pasture took on new and more literal significance. It had been reenacted, or rather *en-acted* collectively for the first time, in the transit of Europeans from the oppressive environment of the Old World to the open, unspoiled terrain of the New. But it often was difficult, if not impossible, to distinguish between elements borrowed from the pastoral (a distinct literary mode), and those which had been more or less spontaneously generated in America—a kind of indigenous pastoralism blended out of evangelical Christianity and the pervasive, if attenuated, myth of America as the land of a new beginning. (The image of America as a "garden," for example, combines Christian and pastoral elements.)[13] I will return to the distinction.

But first, a word should be said about the concept of *myth* as used in American Studies. This is another term that resists precise definition, for it refers to a more complex mental construct that belongs on the continuum, introduced earlier, that leads from image to symbol. If a symbol may be defined as an image invested with significance beyond that required for referential purposes, then a myth is a combination of symbols, held together by a narrative, which embodies the virtually all-encompassing conception of reality—the world-view—of a group. The many versions of the "American myth" embody ideas of the genesis and meaning of the new nation, and according to the pastoral version the Republic was formed as a result of the movement of Europeans across the Atlantic, away from a complex society dominated by the striving for status, wealth and power, to a simpler world of rural peace, sufficiency and virtue. Emigration, as described in the myth, was a voyage of spiritual and political regeneration. But there was no need, in this particular study, to document the hold of the myth upon the American consciousness. On that score the evidence already was overwhelming.[14] In gauging the response to industrialization, however, it became necessary to distinguish between the interpretation of the myth characteristic of the dominant or general culture, and the interpretation of writers like Thoreau and Melville. For this purpose the concept of pastoral, a literary mode with a long and rich history, and the distinction between complex and sentimental kinds of pastoral, proved to be invaluable.

Pastoral conventions often had lent themselves to both serious and sentimental uses. Sophisticated writers working in the mode generally had been careful to surround the arcadian dream with something like irony; they made it difficult, that is, for perceptive readers to come away with a simple belief in idyllic possibilities. But the extraordinary promise of life in America made it relatively easy for indulgent writers to gratify the popular taste for pleasure fantasies. Thus the distinction between complex and sentimental pastoralism helped to illuminate divergent American responses to industrialization in the nineteenth century. To be sure, the image of the machine was incorporated in a pastoral design at all levels of the culture, but there were marked variations in the significance attached to the device at various levels. In the general culture on the whole, the image of the machine in the American landscape was treated as a token of hope and progress. It served, in effect, to endorse the progressive idea of history inherited from the Enlightenment, and to reconcile industrialization with the pastoral myth of a new beginning. Here the industrial power was interpreted, curiously enough, as an instrument for creating the simple, rural society envisaged in the myth. On the other hand, writers like Thoreau and Melville, whose intellectual affinities were with the romantic counter-Enlightenment, turned the device into a dark metaphor of contradiction. For them the sudden appearance of the iron machine in the green landscape evoked a sense of the irreconcilability of the nation's actions and ideals. In their work the image of industrial power, set against the professed desire for rural simplicity, becomes a vehicle for ironic and even tragic pastoralism. It discloses the widening gap between reality and myth which was—and still is—consistently obscured in the general culture.

3. *Conclusion.* With this sample project in view, some of the ways in which the two methods complement each other should be obvious. A striking weakness of the American Studies approach is its imprecise description of the general culture. For this phase of the humanist's work the procedures used by the content analyst in studying public opinion

would seem to be appropriate. Certainly it would be useful to find out whether the techniques of systematic sampling and analysis can provide a more detailed and reliable picture. An experiment in collaboration also should be useful to the social scientist, if only because the insights gained from imaginative literature would be a source of provocative questions, and of significant patterns of meaning not likely to be found in the raw data usually examined by students of public opinion. Just as Freud put literary themes to clinical tests, so the content analyst might check the intuitions of the most talented writers against the accessible facts.

In suggesting the possibility of collaborative effort, however, I would not gloss over the profound gulf between the aims of the two schools, as indicated by the concern of one with "public opinion" and of the other with "culture." To the student of public opinion the important aspect of the American response to industrialization before the Civil War is to be found in documents which express widely held attitudes. His purpose is to understand collective behavior at the time. The opinions that matter most, presumably, are those which made themselves felt in action, and particularly in public affairs. Therefore it is reasonable to regard virtually any political speech or editorial comment made on the subject in 1851 as more significant than, say, *Moby Dick*. No one will deny that at the time such documents had a greater impact upon the collective consciousness, and are more revealing of popular attitudes, than Melville's novel. Why, then, does the humanist working in American Studies consider the novel relevant? On what ground does he take it seriously as a source of insights into the relation between industrialization and mind in nineteenth century America?

The correct answer to this question too often has been obscured by extravagant claims for the value of imaginative literature as historical data. Not only must the humanist grant that *Moby Dick* had no immediate public appeal, but he also should grant that it is no more valuable than many lesser works of fiction as a "reflection" of objective reality. Quite the contrary, so far from crediting the indefensible claim that the best books somehow provide a more reliable mirror image of actuality, that they are more representative of "the spirit of the age," it seems more reasonable to argue that the books of the 1850s which we now value least—the truly popular novels of the age—are the most useful as historical documents of this kind. The writers whose works endure as art tend on the whole to be the most critical of—the most emancipated from—the prevailing culture.

If our purpose is to represent the common life, then we should not turn to the masterpieces we continue to read and enjoy. Probably it would be best, for that purpose, to put literature aside altogether. In any event, and this is the crux of the method being defended here, I would submit that the argument for the usefulness of *Moby Dick* in the kind of inquiry I have described is identical with the argument for the intrinsic merit of *Moby Dick* as a work of literature. It is useful for its satisfying power, its capacity to provide a coherent organization of thought and feeling, or in a word, for its compelling truth value.

But I realize that no social scientist can accept this answer. What objective validation can there be, he asks, for ascribing cognitive value to a work of literature? The answer, of course, is that for the humanist there are no sanctions which can be called objective, which are unmodified by judgments of value. The high value attached to Melville's novel rests upon its continuing—one might say, growing—capacity, as compared with the editorial of 1851, to provide us with satisfaction, and to shape our experience of past and present. At first this may seem to be a simple distinction between the instrumental (or political) value of the editorial and the intrinsic (or esthetic) value of the novel. But even that distinction loses its force when we shift from the immediate perspective of the 1850s to the long-term perspective of the present. For in the longer perspective *Moby Dick* clearly must be credited with having had the greater influence upon American action as well as thought. And yet, to say that the novel had a greater influence *upon* the culture is a misleading way of putting it, for it obscures the literal sense in which the enduring work of art *becomes* the culture which produced it. With the passage of time, that is, books of the stature of *Moby Dick* comprise a larger and larger portion of the consciousness of nineteenth century America that remains effectively alive in the present. The importance we attach to the novel arises, in the last analysis, from the fact that today it is read, studied, and incorporated in our sense of ourselves and of our world, past and present. So far, then, as the book embodies a response to industrialization, it is a particularly significant response—more significant for us than one which may have had a greater influence upon public opinion at the time. But the measure of that significance cannot be located in any objective realm, uncompromised by human judgment. It derives from choices made by human beings, hence they are the ultimate basis for the method we would call humanistic.

Comment 5

◆

Edward Lurie

DEPARTMENT OF HUMANITIES, PENNSYLVANIA STATE MEDICAL SCHOOL, HERSHEY

MARX HAS ATTEMPTED to define two methods of studying the American past, and by implication, the present. He labors in that aspect of the past he designates as "humanist" in its approach. By this I take him to mean that through the use of selected data representative of the "high" culture and its diagrammatic representation, he can construct a "humanist method" to study, assess, and define the relationships between the high and the general culture.

Having foresworn the rigid categories of social science and method, Marx takes refuge in his own devices. But this harsh designation, like the inner light that struck at Jonathan Edwards' psyche, is pure and sweet, because it is humanist and therefore humane. Is it so because it deals with men? If true, I find this puzzling because I always thought that in order to understand any culture one must work with what its *inhabitants* and advocates did, thought, wrote, said, and felt about a congerie of subjects, low, high, middle, or what have you. I think Marx means it is humanist for two more basic reasons. First, the "method" is espoused by that unorganized group who are themselves humanists—that is they generally have doctorates in English or American studies, rather than in sociology, history, anthropology, or folk medicine. Second, it is humane because it deals with the thought of people who, groupy or not, muddied their hands in the unhumanistic business of Ohio ideas, Wyoming society, Brooklyn cultural trends, and the like.

I shall not spend much time evaluating Marx's assessment of the method of content analysis; there are others who are much more capable than I am of doing this. But more important, I agree entirely with his evaluation of it. Content analysis is the worst thing to happen to the study of the American past since John Fiske or Theodore Roosevelt began interpreting it. But I cannot accept the baby of Marx's valid complaint and at the same time buy his bathwater of anti-intellectualism that has nothing but disdain for mere laborers in the transallegheny vineyard of the common man's mind. There is a strong element of disdain for the mere counting of heads in his paper, and in distinction, an equally strong pride in the analysis of bright heads. These heads are designated as brilliant, seemingly, either by the judges of high culture in the past itself (someone like James T. Fields) or his analog in the present (someone like the god of the unorganized eastern methodologists, Edmund Wilson).

There is much talk these days among students, faculty, and advocates of black power, of the need to be "relevant" to the needs, interests, and problems of the disenfranchised, the poor, the *lumpenproletariat* spawned by the modern end to the American dream. Whether or not these pleas are valid, the fact is that Marx's evaluations are *really* irrelevant to the needs of the modern student, teacher, or professor of things-in-general, because they say nothing about what really was, or should have been, or might be. "High-Cult," as I call this attitude, is laden with the very deficiencies in method Marx points to as problematical in his "defense," namely, artificial selectivity, historicism, and unrepresentativeness. If Sir Charles Snow gave the modern world a false dichotomy between science and humanism, Marx has continued such bifurcation by positing a false barrier between humanism and behavioral science, the high and the general culture.

In doing so, however, it is important for Marx to supply an essential and primary justification for his method. But he has not specified the manner in which the humanistic approach fulfills one of its alleged aims, namely, the specification of the relations between existential reality and the collective consciousness, or what he calls the high and the general culture. He has not shown how the concepts of literary art are in fact reinterpreted, reshaped, and syncretized to become part of the larger cultural fabric of a people over a given segment of time. This is a vital endeavor. I can think of nothing more important in the analysis of cultural patterns or history than the tracing of transmission lines, intellectual linkages, processes of dilution or reinterpretation operative between the "thought" of a Newton, for example, the popularizations of a Voltaire, and the thinking about science by wealthy French women of the late eighteenth century who read one of their favorite sages.

At times Marx seems to give the impression that it is not even very important for this effort at syncretism between the high and general cultures to take place at all, because the best works of literary art do not merely *represent* the spirit of the age, they *are* in fact that spirit. Note these phrases:

> The really difficult problem the content analyst faces in dealing with imaginative literature is not the selection but the interpretation of the material. . . . The judgment implicit in the concept of "high" culture marks a crucial distinction between the methods of the humanist and the social scientist. . . . the scholar who is . . . an "expert" in American literature . . . is expert about a relatively small fraction of the whole body of . . . writing. . . . he cannot be said to "know" American writing in the sense of having made an independent selection of the most significant works . . . His inquiry . . . begins with the established canon—a selection . . . based on the collective wisdom, which . . . includes the most fully realized, complex and powerful (hence enduring) work of American writers.

Speaking of his selection of writers for *The Machine in the Garden,* Marx affirms that he hardly needed to work at this at all, but that a kind of invisible hand of God worked its purpose through him: "Their status as 'major' which is to say their place in the 'high' culture *had of course been determined for me* by the conventional literary wisdom" (italics mine). I could go on and on, but the points, as Marx makes them, do little to advance an understanding of the nature of culture. Suppose, for example, that American culture of the mid-nineteenth century was vitally influenced by the culture of Slobovia, and that that culture was distinctly Low-Cult in its forms, manners, and values. If the adherence to "high culture" is held to as the "crucial" distinction between humanistic and behavioral science, then how assess a Gen-Cult impact on a High-Cult culture if the choices for analysis are limited to "conventional literary wisdom." If the conventional wisdom of the Slobovians is interpreted and evaluated for Marx by the designators of Slobovian Low-Cult, "established canons" will not help him assess the ways in which Emerson, Melville, Hawthorne, or Henry James experienced a Slobovian influence in their ideas, because by definition the writing of this genre forms a cultural matrix supreme unto itself. The door to possible reinterpretations based upon research into Slobovian-American cultural interdependence has thus been closed.

This last criticism leads directly to a central deficiency in the analysis. Marx does not tell us how the "spirit of the age" is in fact shaped and determined. When John Higham first designated this phrase as an apt manner of determining, for the purposes of intellectual history, the identification of one culture era contrasted with others, this was an important contribution because it stressed not only a means for definition, but also suggested ways in which such definitions might be sought (this is called "methodology" by social scientists), and also cited the components that might be examined to determine the spirit of an age.[15] At the same time, Howard Mumford Jones suggested there were alternate and more significant temporal and spatial areas that revealed much about ideas in America, in this case in the cultural history of South and Central America.[16] If Jones is correct, and there is much in *O Strange New World* to convince me he is, how does Marx's approach provide the American Studies movement with conceptualizations to subsume the data and the theoretical contributions of the Jones suggestion? It does not and cannot, because it rests on affirmations of humanism and anti-scientism that are not merely anti-intellectual and contemptuous of the lower orders of society, but also embrace a kind of chauvinism that needs to be disputed, especially at this juncture in America's world relationships.

Marx does admit that the proper formulation of the character of the connection between the high culture and the spirit of the age is as yet an unsolved problem. As he well says, the central issue is the establishment of the nexus between the high and the general culture. But if an enduring work of literature ("fiction" is presumably Gen-Cult) receives its value because it is not merely representative but also molds and forms the high culture, how establish the "nexus" between high and general if the two sides of the Marx-made line are qualitatively different? If the character of the spirit of the age is dependent on the high culture that shapes it, then there must be a mode of determining correspondence. A simple law of social science is that one can only compare things that are comparable.[17] But how compare the differential qualities in the cultural matrix that comprise each aspect of this equation? And comparison is vital if the point of correspondence or interaction is to be charted. If, on the other hand, the spirit of an age has a life of *its* own, independent of the high culture towering above it, then the search for correspondence is valueless. All of this would be important to determine if Marx did not continue to interlard his argument with affirmations that documents of high culture do not merely reflect it, they *are* that culture. I find this argument somewhat akin to Aristotle's definition of the effects of opium when he affirmed that the drug made the user drowsy because of its dormative qualities.

Marx is also confused regarding his meaning or definition of culture. Apparently, one interpretation he opts for is Henry Nash Smith's that has culture comprising the examination of the past and present of the phenomena adopted by anthropologists in the late 1930s and early 1940s. But if the study of national culture is to be representational of what is being studied, then the Berlin wall Marx has built separating the high and the general culture must be breached. He has not shown how this piercing may occur. He has not done this, I suspect, because he does not really believe there is always the need to justify the study of American high culture in terms of its significance for understanding the spirit of the age. Marx would, I think, like to read his Hawthorne, Thoreau, and Edith Wharton for their intrinsic literary merit. In fact, he is explicit about this, affirming that the contextual scholars, while seemingly ahistorical, are in fact performing a singular service to history by determining, with the sharpest scrutiny, the exact character of a work of great literature so that "this key doctrine of the allegedly anti-historical 'new criticism' is being incorporated into the essentially historical enterprise of American Studies." I am not a wholly authorized spokesman for the historical profession, but I must say for the record that my own research and writing in American ideas and culture has not been aided in any measure whatsoever by the dedicated men of MLA who labor long and hard to determine the exact number of commas in the original text of *Bartelby the Scrivener* or the precise wording of the original version of *The Turn of the Screw*. Historians have found ample ways to employ public and private funds in the endless editions of the letters of nearly every major and many minor politicians, diplomats, and public men. I see no need why this useless enterprise has to be replicated by the humanist, especially since Marx is right—the "crucial distinction" between the methods of the humanist and the social scientist is that the former deals with the implicit character of high culture, while the latter is relegated to the netherlands of the general, middle, or even low culture. I say that both the historian and literary scholar, social scientist, and humanist who pore over old leavings of the past do so to avoid thinking about them, because they are either lazy or incapable of generalizing about the cultural significance of *Leaves of Grass* or *Deadwood Dick*. Like Bartelby, I would prefer not to enjoy this great contribution to historical understanding.

But there is a more erroneous conception in Marx's attempt to define the character and the significance of the components of the high culture and its relationships to other elements of the intellectual environment. Even though he genuflects before "works of art, music, engineering, political theory, philosophy," and "any creations of man," the implicit assumption of his paper is that literature, and only the best literature selected by the smartest men, is identifiable with high culture. It is one thing to use examples from imaginative expressions, but I take this opportunity to remind scholars that American culture is not comprised of either the be all and end all of Supreme Court decisions or "Great American Novels." Hence a double error is committed: the great middle ground of Mid-Cult is effectively ignored, and worse, Lit-Cult becomes Cult *per se*. Just as Henry Nash Smith found marvelous examples for political history in literary expression, so do scientists and lawyers have minds, and the way they use them determines the shape of their world and our reconstruction of it.

Having failed to supply us with either a scientific or unscientific method for relating one level of culture to another, Marx affirms that American Studies and the movement it symbolizes can in fact make this very real contribution and has in fact made it since about 1946 or 1950. I disagree. Some of my best friends teach American Studies, have doctoral degrees in it, and are presidents or officers of its regional and national associations. Though I teach in such a program, and must confess to organizational and leadership involvement in the business, I really think now that, after more than two decades of existence, the American Studies movement has failed. I know no one who has been formally associated with it, Marx especially, who would not have made singular intellectual contributions as members of English, history, or even sociology and anthropology departments.[18] As a discipline or a movement or what have you, American Studies cannot tell us, or Marx cannot tell us in unauthorized spokesman fashion, the manner for making congruent the varying levels of culture because there is no theoretical or technical contribution in this intellectual construct that will enable him to do so. I say this in full knowledge of the plethora of statements about methodology that advocates of the movement have written. I like their substantive works much better. Hence, in the case of Marx, I find nothing in his paper that is not the work of a careful literary historian with a certain—and highly respectable—point of view toward his craft.

I suggest that we could all save a lot of time if it were rationally admitted that there is no discipline such as American Studies. By discipline I mean an intellectual construct or approach to knowledge that is distinguished by technique ("method") for understanding data, sharing the construction of hypotheses with subject matter analogous though not homologous with it (as in the physical sciences), and advancing generalizations that are testable and can comprise a general theory of being (as in the theory of the nature of the American frontier or the character of organic evolution).

I suggest that despite the fine stimulus given the movement by such men as Howard Mumford Jones, Henry Nash Smith, and Daniel Aaron, American Studies really took hold because it provided a new academic refuge and bastion of prestige to people who did not want to hang on in traditional English and history departments. There was some effort to pay homage to the "new" social sciences, such as anthropology, but this never got much beyond citing the contributions to our understanding of American culture by Ruth Benedict and Margaret Mead. Moreover, academics being what they are in both the nineteenth and twentieth centuries, the movement provided yet another opportunity for societies, journals, conferences, congresses, international alliances, and the like; in short, all the trappings of what Irving Barrett has identified as the deformation of the contemporary American intellectual.

There are certain approaches drawn from the history of intellectual and cultural history in the United States that would be conformable with Marx's concern with developing a technique. But this aspect of historical study is itself almost as deficient as American Studies in its failure to develop a philosophy or method, and its inability to do what Higham and others have asked, to establish viable means for understanding the relationships between literate culture and the total *Zeitgeist* of a period. To marry intellectual history to American Studies is akin to merging Casey Stengel's New York Mets with, say, the old St. Louis Browns. The bad baseball would merely be increased. I suggest that one reason for the inadequacy of American Studies as a significant field of learning is that it traditionally rested upon the all too weak shoulders of American literary history and American intellectual history, neither of which possessed a fully fleshed philosophy or set of working conceptualizations.

Scholars should end their concern with such problems as the differences between the high and the general culture and begin examining a host of meaningful ones whose resolution might advance knowledge. As to method, I think we should follow Satchel Paige's dictum, pronounced when some reporter asked him how he could continue to pitch a baseball so well at his advanced age. "Man, I just stays loose," was the rejoinder, and so should students of the national culture. They should use any technique—content analysis, the new criticism, or environmental analysis —that will unravel some mystery of the past, whether that mystery resides in Brooklyn or Concord. We have tread too long along old and tired paths, bound and fettered by the defense of something that is indefensible, and the result has been a failure of creative imagination.

Finally, I should like to extend Marx's quest into some unexplored areas. His analysis needs to deal with the relationship between democracy and the technique of studying its culture. In the United States intellectual leaders have often felt that they must seek out a high culture or a distinguished kind of intellectual history, even if in fact that cultural existence was far less important than the evaluation attributed to it. Jefferson, Emerson, John Fiske, and Max Lerner are all guilty of this cultural error, an error made because of a basic insecurity with regard to European achievements as compared to American contributions to literature, science, or art. We feel belittled when we have to stack an Emerson or Whitman against a Hegel or Goethe, and so we avidly seek out second and third rate men of the mind and designate them as culture heroes (hence the absorption with Gen-Cult), and at the same time we honor the Franklins and the John Deweys in a pathetic effort to show Europeans we are as good as they. But again, in the effort to compare what is comparable, this procedure is like comparing the New York Mets to the National League All Stars, or the Ohio Academy of Sciences to the Paris Academy of Sciences.

Conversely, students of America feel they must pay some homage to the processes of social democracy in the life of the mind and the concept that knowledge will uplift the common man. In this effort we search for connections between high culture and the spirit of the age, when none in fact exists, so that Willard Gibbs must somehow become part of the spirit of the Gilded Age because the man and the times existed side by side. The same is true with Henry Adams, Santayana, or Charles Saunders Pierce, and the result, as Marx would surely agree, is the failure of the cultural analysts to treat these figures at all intelligently.

It is vital, as John Higham urged, to discover the actual spirit of an age, and as Marx suggests, to do this by evaluations based on some sort of intrinsic as well as extrinsic scale. But this contribution will not be made by taking refuge in the unimaginative approaches followed during the last two decades of national scholarship. Surely we owe something to the generation of students that feel all is irrelevant and meaningless—to show more relevancy and meaning about the intelligence that comprises our cultural bank account.

6

Social scientists, especially those recently converted to behaviorism, often deride what they perceive to be the naive way in which historians gather, present, and analyze their data. They question the ultimate value of a monograph based upon invisible coding rules and intuitive sampling procedures. Above all, they impugn the credibility of a discipline which apparently revels in the fact that two different scholars looking at the same body of evidence often reach diametrically opposed conclusions. Many social scientists feel that this distressing situation can be remedied by the historian's adoption of such modern techniques as empirical content analysis.

One reason why historians have been unwilling to experiment with content analysis is because they do not understand the mysteries of chi squares and two-tailed tests. While manuals on content analysis are available for inspection, few relate directly to the unique problems of the historian. Richard L. Merritt content analyzed colonial American newspapers in Symbols of American Community *(1966). Although he did ask questions of relevance to historians, he did not write the volume with the historical community in mind. Thus, in this paper Merritt describes as simply as possible the steps involved in undertaking a similar project of interest to historians.*

John Higham weighs the merits of such an approach for members of his craft. The author of Strangers in the Land *(1955) and* History *(1965), Higham has long been concerned with problems in historical theory and methodology.*

Perspectives on History
In Divided Germany

◆

Richard L. Merritt

DEPARTMENT OF POLITICAL SCIENCE, UNIVERSITY OF ILLINOIS

POLITICAL CONSIDERATIONS dictated the reform of Germany's educational system after the collapse of Nazism in the spring of 1945. The governments of postwar Germany, no less than the victorious Allies of World War II, who exerted absolute control over the country for more than four years, realized full well the importance of education in forming the ideas and behavior of a nation.[1] It is, to be sure, not the only element. The family, playground, peer group, and workplace each plays its role in the process of political socialization. But in the political reconstruction of Germany, the educational system seemed a good place to start. For one thing, there was the naive belief that formal schooling plays the *key* role in the building of citizens, that, if it can be changed, this in turn would have an impact upon other aspects of the socialization process. For another thing, the school system is something that can be taken by the hand and molded, whereas other elements, such as the family, are less subject to external influences. It is possible to reform curricula, to weed out teachers objectionable because of their political taint, to introduce practices such as student government, and even to rewrite textbooks.

The country's division in 1948 and the subsequent development of the Federal Republic of Germany (FRG) in the West and the German Democratic Republic (GDR) in the East created two separate educational systems as well.[2] They were nonetheless related in several regards. The language of education, for instance, remained German. At the time this was certainly not remarkable. Since then, however, the differential impact of political ties—new concepts and terms peculiar to the different political systems; Russian as the first foreign language in the GDR schools, and English or French in the FRG schools—together with two decades of separate lives and concerns, has produced the beginnings of what may blossom into a linguistic schism. Second, a common educational tradition pervaded both systems. The GDR has gone furthest in altering this tradition. (Its centralized school system contrasts sharply with the dozen differing systems controlled by the individual states in the FRG.) Its common, polytechnic schools have replaced the complicated structure of types of schools that still characterizes the FRG. Third, the subject matter of education has remained the same.

Or has it? The coldest of cold warriors would agree that two plus two equals four, that most cows have four legs and a tail, that the 1848 Revolution took place in 1848. But whether the student computes compound interest on investments or the output of a collectivized farm during his arithmetic class, whether or not he studies Lysenko's theories of genetics in biology courses, whether or not he spends much time reading and discussing the works of Karl Marx—all these are ultimately political questions. The selection and presentation of the subject matter of education are fraught with political implications.

In few areas is this truer than in the study of history. Our images, attitudes, and values shape our approach to the past. And in turn our knowledge of past events and the theories we use to interpret them are crucial to our view of the world around us and to our behavior toward it. In giving school children a selective presentation and interpretation of past events—of the causes and consequences of imperialism, for instance, or the role of the working class in national development—we are in effect giving them a guide to life in our own world of images, attitudes, and values. Indeed, this is one of the traditional functions of education, one that was instrumental in many arguments for the extension of free, popular education.[3] In the fulfillment of this function, history texts, too, have their part to play.

The essence of writing history is systematic simplification. No writer can cover every conceivable aspect of his subject. Instead, he selects the events that he will explore according to criteria of relevance resting upon conscious or unconscious assumptions about the nature of his subject. Ideally, but not always, the historian states his criteria at the outset of his work, thereby enabling the reader to evaluate his writing properly, and adheres to them throughout the study. More frequently the underlying and even implicit values of the writer's society color his approach. And sometimes he writes in a way that deliberately disguises his true criteria of relevance. When George Orwell, in his futuristic novel *1984*, discussed the rewriting of history to conform to current concerns and views—a refashioning of the past that creates historical personages or obliterates them by turning them into "unpersons"—he was merely magnifying a process that goes on daily in every country, although usually with far less diabolical goals in mind. Still, it is characteristic of totalitarian societies that they seek to create a body of historical literature that proceeds from a set of (generally unstated) premises, but under sufficient control that it does not contain internal contradictions or information which would lead the uncritical reader to question the premises.

The comparative evaluation of written history requires a delineation of its systematic aspect. If we can be sure that the set of assumptions from which the author proceeded is the same as our own, then our criticism may be fairly simple. Are the author's historical data accurate? Does he take account of conflicting data? Has he included relevant items and excluded the irrelevancies? Is his interpretation "reasonable" in the sense that it follows the canons of logical analysis and takes account of other and possibly contradictory interpretations? If, however, we know or suspect the writer started from a set of assumptions we do not share, then our task is considerably different. A critique of Marxist history from a "Western liberal" point of view may be accurate but, unless it considers the differing perspectives, it may well be beside the point as far as the study itself is concerned. In such cases genuine communication breaks down. The initial task of historical criticism, then, is to determine the perspectives shaping the writer's approach to the past. Until we know them, it makes little sense to discuss the writer's ability to gather information, to organize it coherently, and to draw conclusions.

The Presentation of History in German Schools

This paper reports some detective work on the perspectives of East and West German writers of history textbooks aimed at the senior high school level. Its specific purpose is to determine the extent to which varying pictures of the world and its history confront advanced students in the two parts of Germany. To the extent that the educational systems propagate varying views, and to the extent that other aspects of the socialization process reinforce what is taught in the schools, young people will develop varying perspectives. To the extent that the varying perspectives are incompatible, but rewarding for those holding them, they will produce divergencies within the population. Over the long run, their snowballing effect begins to encompass aspects of life other than perspectives on past events. And in extreme cases the consequence may be the development of separate "national" identities.

The Uses of History Texts. History textbooks offer a wealth of possibilities for analyzing societal perspectives. The fact that they comprise a standardized means for socializing students means that they can give us important clues about the content of that socialization process. Moreover, they are readily available for various types of analysis. Yet at the same time there are dangers in their use. For one thing, the textbook author is a mediator transmitting aspects of the culture to a particular audience. There are several points in the process of transmitting perspectives at which errors of one sort or another can creep in. An author, for instance, has a wide stock of historical information available to him when he sits down to write. On what basis does he make his selection of events to relate? Can we safely conclude that his vision of cultural values is reasonably accurate? For another thing—and this point is more relevant for the United States than for Germany—the process by which textbooks are prepared for school use is complicated. There are several factors that help to determine what textbooks a committee of the school board may choose: contracts between publishers and particular writers, copyrights and copyright infringements, production costs, marketing considerations, regional differentiation (how likely is it that a textbook manufacturer will be able to sell to a school board in Mississippi a book which pictures white and black children playing together?), personal relationships between salesmen and school board members in particular areas, and so forth. Even the textbook most representative of cultural values can easily fall into a trap somewhere along this route. In the German case, where the individual states control the selection of textbooks for classroom use, this problem of representativeness is not severe.

Another limitation must be perfectly clear at the outset. What appears in textbooks may represent the formally approved view of events and processes, but their content alone tells us little about what was actually communicated to students. First, students read the texts in conjunction with classroom lectures and discussions. If the individual instructor stresses a set of perspectives at variance with those in the text (and to be perfectly cynical for a moment, if the instructor is also the man who examines and grades the students), then it is questionable how much of the book's content his students will absorb. We have no control over the totality of what is taught in the classroom. Second, students usually have sources of perspectives outside the school's halls. This, of course, is a particular problem in countries such as the GDR, in which the government is trying to educate students along lines that are at odds with what their parents were taught to believe. Similarly, the views presented by friends, in books and movies, and by such institutions as the church, compete for the student's attention. Finally, even if we had perfect information about the congruent and conflicting messages communicated to the student, we have precious little information about their effect. How much of what is communicated actually catches his attention? How much of that does he absorb? What standards does he use to evaluate competing messages? Even if it should turn out that there is a high degree of congruence between what is taught and what is internalized (as indicated, for example, through surveys), how sure can we be that there is a direct causal relationship? In short, the content of history texts can at best serve as an indicator of the formal socialization process that students encounter. But, it must be added, it remains one of the best such indicators available to scholars.

Varieties of Content. The analysis of German texts takes place on two levels. The first is the open or *manifest* content of the texts: the image of past events (e.g., "Bismarck made public a falsified version of the Ems Dispatch," "The Socialist Law of 1878 banned the Social Democratic Party from German political life"); attitudes expressed toward events, institutions, or persons ("Bismarck was a great political leader," "Social Democracy was the hope of the working class, and its salvation"); and basic political values ("Bismarck's greatness lay in his furtherance of German national interests," "The working class should have the machinery to control its own destiny"). The overt perspectives that the student carries with him from his education are those that he is likely to recall in response to specific stimuli. Consider for example the differential view of postwar Germany's rearmament. The text currently in use in East Berlin stresses that the creation of a National People's Army in the GDR was a response to remilitarization in West Germany. West Berlin's history book, by way of contrast, saw the earlier formation in East Germany of People's Police units stationed in army-like bases as grounds contributing to the decision to create the Federal Army. At the very least, those taking stock in these varying beliefs will find communication on this topic difficult. A thorough contextual analysis of East and West German textbooks with a view toward delineating areas of agreement and disagreement on perspectives would be valuable.[4] This report focuses more upon the underlying or *latent* content of the textbooks—the message communicated to the reader through the tone and style of the writing. This could include levels of affect. When an East German text, for example, states that to put down the workers' revolution in 1848, "the bourgeoisie created a special police force out of vagabonds and shirkers," it is more than a mere statement that the police formed auxiliary units to assist them! It could also include levels of activity—whether the police arrived to restore order or rushed to quell the revolution.[5]

Of particular interest in this paper is the question: Who participated in history? Who were the actors during the course of a particular event—such as the Revolution of 1848, the formation of the Reich in 1871, the decision to go to war in 1914, the division of Germany in 1945-1949— and who were those acted upon? On the one hand, as suggested earlier, the writer of history can color his narrative account through the systematic selection of certain types of heroes. Nazism, for instance, glorified a set of men of whom few had heard anything prior to 1933 and who are mostly forgotten now. Horst Wessel, a young Nazi killed during street fighting with the Left, became fabled in song and story; but in modern Germany he remains only as a symbol of a shameful past. If two writers with a common background but with differing perspectives write a history of that background, they may unconsciously discuss markedly different casts of characters. The believer writing of Christianity in ancient Rome may identify with the martyrs thrown to the lions in the arena; the agnostic classicist may be interested in these early Christians only as a phenomenon affecting social stability in Rome (to my knowledge no one as yet has identified with the lions—with the possible exception of George Bernard Shaw!). "Who Whom?" as Lenin phrased it in his famous pamphlet of 1902, is a crucial question in historical writing. But the way in which it is answered also has important implications for our perspectives regarding modern life. If history is seen as a battle of giants against one another, then we, as average citizens, can sit back to watch the show going on now. If, however, history is the story of how various groups or classes of men tugged and pulled against one another, then what the common man acting in a group does is important.

Concentration upon varying perspectives in modern East and West Germany naturally leads us to inquire about their antecedents. Hence a secondary purpose of this paper is to examine the sources of current perspectives. If in fact there are differences between East and West, can we trace them to earlier periods in German historiography? Do they differ more from each other than either of them does from the set of perspectives offered to Germans of earlier generations? To find the answer to such questions, it seemed necessary to analyze comparable textbooks of history from the era of the Wilhelmine Reich, the Weimar Republic, and the twelve years of the National Socialist Third Reich that was to last a thousand years.

The Focus on Events: The 1848 Revolution. Two practical considerations dictated the decision to examine actors participating in specific historical events. The first of these was the sheer impracticability of analyzing in any systematic manner the whole of history as presented in German textbooks of varying eras. The second was, since the whole of history is compressed into a thousand or less pages, that any random system proved to be too likely to catch discussions of unrelated events. It seems reasonable, to take an absurd example, to expect that a discussion of the Napoleonic wars would not pay much attention to Bismarck. And yet a random selection of pages dealing with history in the nineteenth century might well concentrate upon the Napoleonic wars in one text, and upon the Bismarck era in another, thereby giving rise to differences that would be artifactual rather than real.

The criteria for selecting appropriate events were several. First, the events should be important for German history. Thus international diplomacy, such as that of the Crimean War, would not be directly relevant. Second, the events must be discussed in all texts. This limits the selection as far as East German texts are concerned, for they tend to discuss events that are not mentioned in other histories (particularly those of the Wilhelmine Reich). It also limits selections from the earliest books, for some events reported there proved over the course of the years to be too insignificant to rate space in later histories. Third, at least one set of events should be in the postwar era, more directly relevant to the separate courses of history in East and West Germany. Naturally, for these events we would have no comparative point in past German historiography. Fourth, the events should be episodes comprising series of discrete events and actions. They should be roughly definable, that is, with a beginning and end, and with a sequence upon which there is general agreement. In this sense the "emergence of nationalism" is too amorphous. Finally, the events should involve action. Hence a discussion of Hegel's philosophy or Dürer's art is not pertinent. It must be added that this criterion reduces the validity for the history book as a whole of a systematic analysis of individual events reported in it. For comparative purposes, however, it serves the goal of maximizing the output in terms of the amount of time spent in analysis.

This paper presents the analysis of a single event as a pilot project: the Revolution of 1848. This is not the place to give a detailed history of its causes and sequences, but a brief chronology may serve to refresh the memory:[6]

> 1846–47. France: Food shortages and popular unrest about right to vote lead to street fighting in Paris.
>
> Feb. 1848. Louis Philippe flees to England; Republic is established but its inability to solve economic and employment problems results in uprising on 23 June.
>
> News of events in Paris encourages meetings in Germany; people calmed with promises of new freedoms and constitutions; "March Ministers" appointed in smaller states; uprisings throughout Europe, especially in Milan, Venice, and Hungary.
>
> 13 Mar. 1848. Fall of Metternich in Austria.
>
> 18 Mar. 1848. Mass demonstrations in Berlin.
>
> 1 Apr. 1848. "Demands of the Communist Party in Germany" (Marx and Engels).

31 Mar. to 3 Apr. 1848. *Vorparlament* in Frankfurt discusses the creation of a National Assembly; elections held in all German states.

18 May 1848. National Assembly meets in Paulskirche in Frankfurt to draft constitution; struggle between those wanting greater Germany with Austria against those wanting smaller Germany under Prussia, without Austria; announcement on 27 Dec. of Declaration of Fundamental Rights.

22 May 1848. Prussian National Assembly created to draft constitution; dissolved in Dec.

14 June 1848. Zeughaus Battle in Berlin about demands for arms and disappointment in Prussian Assembly; in Sept. Friedrich Wilhelm IV calls for troops to surround Berlin.

18 Sept. 1848. Street fighting in Frankfurt in response to National Assembly's acceptance of ceasefire in Aug. between Prussia and Denmark on Schleswig-Holstein issue.

Sept. 1848. Hungarian revolutionaries defeat Austrian army; Windischgrätz puts down demonstrations in Vienna in Oct.; Ferdinand I abdicates in favor of 18-year-old Franz Josef in Dec.; proclamation of independent Republic of Hungary on 14 Apr. 1849; Russians aid Austrians between May and Aug. 1849 in putting down Hungarian uprising.

28 Mar. 1849. Frankfurt National Assembly elects Friedrich Wilhelm IV as German emperor; he rejects the crown; further uprisings in Dresden, Baden, and the Palatinate; after moving to Stuttgart in May, remainder of National Assembly disbands in June.

26 May 1849. Creation of Prussian Union Parliament by Friedrich Wilhelm IV.

29 May 1849. Punctation of Olmütz between Prussia and Austria: Prussia gives up Union Parliament and permits reorganization of Bundestag under Austrian domination; Prussia also withdraws troops from Hesse and ultimately from Schleswig-Holstein, leaving the latter to Denmark.

In subsequent research I hope to investigate varying perspectives toward such events as the formation of the Reich in 1871, German imperial policy under Wilhelm II, the outbreak of World War I, the Weimar Republic, Nazism, the postwar Allied occupation, and the division of Germany. The focus in this paper on the Revolution of 1848 will nonetheless serve to demonstrate some of the possibilities and limitations of the approach.

Content Analyzing the Texts. Precisely how to go about analyzing the content of the texts' presentation of the 1848 Revolution poses difficult decisions. What I sought was a procedure simple enough that any scholar or graduate student could apply it in his own research without needing extensive financial support, statistical skills, or access to electronic equipment. To be perfectly frank, since my primary concern is underlying rather than manifest perspectives, the computerized General Inquirer system would have been most nearly ideal from the point of view of thoroughness.[7] Its drawbacks, however, are several. For one thing, in its current stage of development its application is as time consuming as it is expensive. For another, it uses as its starting point an *a priori* analytical framework (e.g., Charles E. Osgood's "semantic differential," Talcott Parsons' "pattern variables," or Harold D. Lasswell's "value configurative" approach) that may be only more or less appropriate for the task at hand. Besides, at this point the General Inquirer is not operational in the German language, and translating the texts was not feasible for a variety of reasons. With luck the situation may improve, but right now the commitment that the scholar who uses the General Inquirer must make in terms of time and resources is forbidding.

Instead, I decided to explore the possibilities of a method of hand coding, outlined in detail in the next section. In brief, this method transforms the sentences as printed in the texts into one or more declaratory statements comprising an actor, the action, and the object acted upon (if any). It classifies the actors further into various types: individuals, groups, institutions, and so forth. Recording this information on punchcards enables rapid analysis not only of the emphasis in the different texts on various types of actors, but also of the who-whom relationship.

Whatever its usefulness—and this will be suggested in a later section of this paper—the method clearly leaves much to be desired. The historian may find that it tells him nothing salient about the event itself, about the Revolution of 1848. The value of the method lies elsewhere. It is not the historical accuracy of the presentation that is of interest but rather the perspectives evident in the writer's perception of the event. In a sense we are looking at the writer's icons in an effort to learn something about his iconography (not about the persons represented by the icons). We want to know something about the values that went into his views of his world. If we assume that the textbook writer is representative of the culture within which he writes, then the values that he presents may be said to reflect those of his culture. More painful is the fact that the method reduces richness of detail and subtleness of style—both of which can clearly be politically relevant—into simple action-oriented assertions. In this regard it ignores crucial aspects of the latent messages communicated by the textbooks. Actors and actor-object relationships are nonetheless important. If this method can tell us something about them, then at least we have made some progress in delineating the complex of underlying perspectives. Finally, the more abstract the level of writing, the less useful this method is likely to be. German high school textbooks are written in terms of who did what, when, how, and occasionally why. The deeper meaning of the actions and events recorded is most frequently left untouched. For this type of writing the method can be valuable; for philosophies of history, additional experimentation would have to test its effectiveness. In short, the particular variety of content analysis used in this paper does not slay all the dragons we can imagine. It nonetheless makes a start, giving us some useful indicators of underlying values in German history texts.

A Design for Research

The decision to analyze the discussion of the 1848 Revolution as it appears in several texts over time poses a number of subsequent decisions. What texts are most appropriate? How do we go about breaking down complex sentences into simple action-oriented assertions? How should we classify the actors? And how can we best organize the data for rapid analysis?

The Selection of History Texts. The criterion governing the selection of textbooks for analysis was their actual use in the different school systems. Where several books were in use, the reputation of their authors was used as an additional criterion.

The task of selecting texts proved difficult for the earlier periods. Not only did several textbooks compete with each other for classroom adoption but, in addition, some of these are no longer readily available, either because of a lack of interest in putting such writings into libraries or because of war-related damage (purposeful destruction during the early Nazi period or during the postwar occupation, bombing of libraries and archives, and the division of Germany, which left considerable material in East German libraries). The fact that the Prussian government published in 1906 a list of schoolbooks acceptable for use in its schools facilitated the search for a book representative of the Wilhelmine period.[8] Of those listed and still available, the most appropriate appeared to be that by Friedrich Neubauer, at that time director of the Royal *Gymnasium* and *Realschule* in Landsberg, and two years later director of the Lessing Gymnasium in Frankfurt am Main, where he remained until his retirement in 1926. Neubauer's own area of concentration was the early nineteenth century in Germany (and particularly Freiherr von Stein). He subsequently became president of the Association of German History Teachers. The success of Neubauer's five-volume history is indicated by the fact that its 25th printing (by this time in its fourth edition) in 1922 brought to 100,000 the number printed and sold.

> 1. Wilhelmine Reich. Friedrich Neubauer, *Lehrbuch der Geschichte für höhere Lehranstalten*, V. Teil: *Vom westfälischen Frieden bis auf unsere Zeit* (Oberprima), 4th print. (Halle a.d. S., Verlag der Buchhandlung des Waisenhauses, 1903): 139–47.

The continuity of Neubauer's book suggested that it might be a useful text for the Weimar period as well. An analysis of this text would at least show us changes in the perspectives of a writer over the period of two decades (and after a disastrous world war). A glance at the treatment in the two books of the 1848 Revolution, however, indicated that there was very little to distinguish them. Hence it made sense to search the list of approved books to find another history text that might be more representative of the Weimar period itself.[9] The ravages of time and war that eliminated many another history text from modern Germany's libraries fortunately preserved that by Franz Schnabel. One of Germany's leading scholars and a member of the German Academy of Sciences, he authored more than a score of books. The Nazis dismissed him from his post as professor at the Karlsruhe Institute of Technology in 1936, but after the war he resumed his academic activities, even bringing out a new edition of his four-volume history of nineteenth century Germany.

> 2. Weimar Republic I. Friedrich Neubauer, *Lehrbuch der Geschichte für höhere Lehranstalten*, V. Teil: *Von der französischen Revolution bis auf unsere Zeit* (Für die Oberprima der höheren Knabenschulen und der Studienanstalten), ed. D, 25th print. of overall ed. (Halle a.d. S., Verlag der Buchhandlung des Waisenhauses, 1922): 91–99.

> 3. Weimar Republic II. Franz Schnabel, *Geschichte der neuesten Zeit: Von der französischen Revolution bis zur Gegenwart: 1789–1919,* 6th print. (Leipzig, B. G. Teubner, 1928): 70–79.

Somewhat more problematic was finding a book for the Nazi era, in part because of Allied ordinances in the immediate post-war period which had required the destruction of surviving copies of books published between 1933 and 1945. The selection of the text by Walther Gehl nonetheless seemed satisfactory. Gehl himself was a champion of the Third Reich, and for its earlier years at least, its chronologer and historian. His published books include *The National Socialist State* (1933), *The National Socialist Revolution, 1914–1932* (1936), *The Years I–IV of the National Socialist State* (1937), and *The Mission of the Reich* (1941). The text, in contrast to the more differentiating volumes by Neubauer and Schnabel, has an almost breezy narrative style, with few dates and no marginal notes. It appears to be free of the more blatant type of Nazi propaganda (although it must be added, Gehl was careful to note who was Jewish and to stress such concepts as "Greater Germany").

> 4. National Socialism. Walther Gehl, *Geschichte: Von der deutschen Ostsiedlung bis zum Scheitern der Märzrevolution* (7. Klasse: Oberschulen, Gymnasien und Oberschulen in Aufbauform) (Breslau, Ferdinand Hirt, 1940): 242–48.

A new style of book production characterizes postwar Germany, both East and West. Typical of this period are collective authorship and domination of the market by few texts. In West Germany two history books enjoy ascendancy. The one used in West Berlin is under the general editorship of eight extremely prominent historians (including Hans Herzfeld, Gerhard Ritter, and Franz Schnabel) and by now is in the sixth printing of the second edition.[10] Its pages are packed with information written up in a tight style—no pictures (other than an occasional photograph of a work of art) or maps, but much background material with reference both to specific events and to the art and culture of the era under discussion. Its description of events presents both sides of the picture, its characterizations of men list both their good and their bad qualities.

> 5. West Berlin. G. Bonwetsch, J. Dittrich, H. H. Eberle, K. Krüger, E. Wilmanns, and G. Wilmanns, *Grundriss der Geschichte für die Oberstufe der höheren Schulen,* II: *Vom späten Mittelalter bis zur Mitte des 19. Jahrhunderts,* ed. B, 6th print. (Stuttgart, Ernst Klett Verlag, 1966): 215–27.

East Berlin (and indeed the entire GDR) uses a single series of graded textbooks for all schools. In contrast to the other texts (including even that by Gehl), the East Berlin series has a clear message that it is trying to convey to its readers: the class basis of social life. The volume covering the period in question begins with a clearcut statement of class distinctions existing in society at that time. And discussion questions at the end of each section almost all relate to these class distinctions and their impact. Particularly interesting is its colorful word usage; and numerous pictures support the text, as do facsimiles of documents and occasional maps.[11]

> 6. East Berlin. Horst Bartel (collective leader), Hans-Jürgen Arendt, Ruth Fuchs, Willibald Gutsche, Rolf Kuntsch, Joachim Müller, Wolfgang Schröder, Gustav Seeber, Kurt Stenkewitz, and Walter Wittwer, *Lehrbuch für Geschichte* (8. Klasse, Oberschule) (Berlin, Volk und Wissen Volkseigener Verlag, 1966): 29–59.

Forming Action-Oriented Assertions. Since the central focus of the paper is variation in the perception of participants in history—who were the initiators and objects of action—it was necessary to reduce all sentences appearing in the relevant portions of the texts to action-oriented assertions. Such assertions have as their subject the actor, that is, whoever or whatever is initiating the action. The predicate is the verb, or nature of the action. And the object is that person, group, or thing that is acted upon. This sounds simple enough. In practice, however, we encountered a number of serious obstacles, mostly of a grammatical nature.

> 1. Sentences with two objects for the same verb were made into two sentences and when necessary a second verb was supplied:
>   a. "Germany defeated Austria and Denmark" becomes
>   i. *Germany* defeated *Austria*[12]
>   ii. *Germany* defeated *Denmark*
>   b. "The Government created national workshops for the unemployed" becomes
>   i. *Government* created *national-workshops*
>   ii. *Government* helped *unemployed*

> 2. In sentences having an accusative object, which in turn has a genitive attribute that does not stem from the verb, the accusative together with its genitive were treated as a single object:
>   a. "The proletariat destroyed the state machine of the exploiter class" becomes—*Proletariat* destroyed *exploiter-class-state-machine*

b. "The collapse of the efforts toward union shook the position of Prussia" becomes—*Union-efforts-collapse* shook *Prussia-position*

3. If the accusative object having a genitive attribute stems from an intransitive verb, with no possibility of having an object, then the accusative and its genitive attribute were likewise left as a unit:
   a. "Prussia agreed to the meeting of the Bundestag" becomes—*Prussia* agreed to *Bundestag-meeting*
   b. "Feudalism hindered the development of industry" becomes—*Feudalism* hindered *industry-development*

4. If the accusative object having a genitive attribute stems from a transitive verb which has or might have an object, then the phrase is broken down into two or more assertions and an object supplied from the context where necessary:
   a. "The Hungarians revolted against Austrian rule" becomes
      i. *Austria* rules *Hungarians*
      ii. *Hungarians* revolt against *rule*
   b. "The Revolution influenced the peoples' wars of liberation" becomes
      i. *Revolution* influenced *liberation-wars*
      ii. *Peoples* wanted to free selves from *Habsburgs* (taken from context)

It must be noted again that, since the orientation of the project comprises actors and action, it seemed desirable to construct separate action-oriented assertions for each actor appearing in the text. Hence "peoples" is made the subject of its own assertion, rather than merely a part of an object (e.g., "peoples'-liberation-wars").

5. If the accusative object having a genitive attribute stems from a verb whose logical subject is the subject of the sentence, the sentence is reconstituted as follows:
   a. "The liberal government took over the administration of Baden" becomes—*Liberal government* began to govern *Baden*
   b. "The Bundestag put on its agenda the revision of the constitution" becomes—*Bundestag* promises to revise *constitution*
   c. "The nation state should reject the oppression of minorities" becomes—*Nation-state* should not oppress *minorities*

6. If the accusative object having a genitive attribute stems from a verb whose subject is not the subject of the sentence, the sentence is reconstituted as follows:
   a. "The workers demanded the revision of the constitution" becomes
      i. *Workers* demand *revision*

ii. *Bundestag* should revise *constitution*
b. "Laws limited railway construction" becomes
   i. *Laws* limit *construction*
   ii. *Capitalists* wanted to build *railways*
c. "The electoral laws enabled no influence upon the government" becomes
   i. *Electoral-laws* enabled no *influence*
   ii. *Population* could not influence *government*

7. As a rule, adverbial phrases are reconstituted, and missing subject, action word, or object supplied:
  a. "Under Napoleon's bondage, the bourgeoisie developed a national consciousness" becomes
   i. *Napoleon* put in bondage *Germany*
   ii. *Bourgeoisie* developed *national-consciousness*
  b. "The Republican Party under Hecker attempted a revolt" becomes
   i. *Hecker* led *Republican-Party*
   ii. *Republican-Party* attempted *revolt*

8. Passive forms, in which the initiator of the action is not mentioned, must be completed. Where the actor cannot be identified with a high degree of certainty, but where he is of considerable importance, the missing element is replaced by the word "Unknown" followed by two asterisks:
  a. "Robert Blum was shot according to martial law" becomes— *Soldiers* shot *Robert-Blum*
  b. "In Vienna, the German flag was hauled down" becomes—*Unknown* hauled down *flag* [actor unimportant]
  c. "A National Assembly was convened" becomes—*Unknown*** convened *National-Assembly* [it might be important to know whether it had been convened by the king or the government, or perhaps by a revolutionary group]

9. Participles:
  a. Present participles are ignored since they are purely attributive: peaceloving citizens, ruling class
  b. Past participles from intransitive verbs are also ignored: sunken ship
  c. No general rule can be made for past participles from transitive verbs; each case must be decided separately according to whether (i) a condition is being described or (ii) the initiator of the condition is also of significance:
   i. interests of the privileged nobility; poorly armed mob
   ii. causes of increased oppression becomes (in part) *bourgeois-government* increased *oppression*

10. Verbs such as own, have, be, become, show, and mean do not take objects involving an action on the part of a subject (as defined in this study); sentences with such verbs are not reconstituted, and may easily be identified in the analysis stage.

11. Some words that are objects in the grammatical sense are not objects or products of an action, but rather part of that action. In general, they may even be changed into verbs without much trouble. Unlike the sentence, "The people demand reform," in which *reform* is clearly the object of the verb *demand,* the following examples show how the object and verb may be combined to create a single verb form:

    a. "The people make demands" becomes—*People* demand

    b. "The King lays down his crown" becomes—*King* abdicates

12. Cities and states used as adverbs are ignored: "Louis Philippe went into exile in England." If, however, they are the object of an action they must be counted as objects:

    a. "The Austrian army occupied Hungary" becomes—*Austria-army* occupied *Hungary*

    b. "General Wrangel announced the siege of Berlin" becomes

        i. *General-Wrangel* announced *siege*

        ii. *General-Wrangel* besieged *Berlin*

13. In those instances where the grammatical subject is not the same as the initiator of the action, the sentence must be reorganized:

    a. "The workers suffered from the economic crisis" becomes—*Economic-crisis* makes suffer *workers*

    b. "The kingdom suffered a defeat at the hands of the mobs" becomes —*Mobs* defeated *kingdom*

    c. "Austria got a constitution" becomes (from context)

        i. *National-Assembly* worked out *constitution*

        ii. *National-Assembly* formed politically *Austria*

14. In idiomatic phrases, where two terms or objects refer to the same verb, the sentence is broken down into two sentences and, where necessary, a second verb is supplied:

    a. "The National Assembly declared Germany a republic" becomes

        i. *National-Assembly* creates *republic*

        ii. *National-Assembly* transforms *Germany*

    b. "Louis Napoleon named himself Emperor of the French" becomes

        i. *Louis-Napoleon* appoints *Emperor-of-French*

        ii. *Louis-Napoleon* appoints *Louis-Napoleon* (himself)

15. If a subject or an object is followed by a prepositional phrase, a second sentence must be formed to include this phrase:

    a. "Marx demanded the unity of the working class and peasants" becomes
      i. *Marx* demanded *unity*
      ii. *Working-class* should unite with *peasants*
    b. "The police regiment created an alienation between the government and the people" becomes
      i. *Police-regiment* created *alienation*
      ii. *Government* alienated itself from *people*

The above list of problems and provisional solutions to them is far from complete. As the method is applied further, it will doubtless encounter many more. The above list can nonetheless serve as an indication of how such issues can be resolved.

Classifying Actors. Actors in history, that is, either the initiators or objects of action, were divided into eleven discrete categories:

    1. *Individual: Official Representative.* This category includes individuals, such as the king or prime minister, acting in their official capacity. In the statement, "Franz Josef succeeded Ferdinand I," neither man is acting in a private capacity. Similarly, when Friedrich Wilhelm agreed to the Punctation of Olmütz, he did so not as an individual but as a representative of the Prussian state. As a counter-example, in the statement, "Ludwig I loved art," Ludwig I would not be considered an official representative (although, depending on the context, in some instances his love of art may be a state act as well).

    2. *Individual: Private Person.* The representatives at St. Paul's Church, such as Von Gagern, Simson, Uhland, and Arndt, were in principle there as representatives of no one but themselves; also included in this category are such persons as Marx and Engels, as well as such leaders of the revolution in the south of Germany as Hecker and Struve.

    3. *Social Group: Membership Organization.* The criterion for this category was the degree of organization of the social group and its cohesiveness. Thus the *Vorparlament* was a membership organization in the sense that membership was a result of conscious behavior, and so was the League of Communists, a trade union, a workers' association, and delegates to a parliamentary conference.

    4. *Social Group: Nationality or Subnationality.* In addition to nationalities named by name, this category includes the term "people" (*Volk*) when it is clear that it refers to the entire nation and not just to a collection of individuals gathered together in one place.

    5. *Social Group: Indeterminate Membership.* Social classes—bougeoisie,

nobility, proletariat—as well as all other aggregates without clearcut member-ship procedures are included here. Examples include the "people" when the term is used to characterize a mere aggregate of individuals, demonstrators, revolutionaries; the clerical party, republican, small-German, or great-German parties; the right or center in reference to political groupings that had no organization in a modern sense. The "revolutionary army" is also included, since these groups were created, not from soldiers or parts of regiments which joined the revolutionaries, but from foreign volunteers and armed civilians.

6. *Nation-state, City, or Other Territorial Unit.* In addition to states (e.g., Prussia), subnational units (e.g., Schleswig), and cities (e.g., Berlin), this category includes such terms as the "middle states" and the "small states" (the referents of which are clear in context), as well as "the Habsburgs" when the term is synonymous with the Austrian state and not the royal family.

7. *Political Institution.* This category contains references to state organiza-tions or agencies, constitutions, armies, police, courts, chambers, and so forth. Although it does not include the term "revolutionary army" (see category 5 above), it does include the "militia" which, during the course of the revolu-tion, attained the status of an official institution.

8. *Abstract Forces of History.* Included in this category are such terms as centralism, particularism, absolutism, industrialization, revolution (but only when it is used in a very general sense—which actually occurred only in the text from East Berlin), and the monarchy (again, only when used in a general sense, and not in reference to a particular monarch, state, or govern-ment).

9. *Impersonal Objects or Events.* Among the terms put into this category were moment, contradiction, braid, pictures, spirit, sacrament, trust, desire, weakness, élan, experience, barricades, and castle.

10. *Political Objects or Events.* The most essential characteristic of the terms included in this category is that they denote politically relevant objects or events that cannot be classified into any of the other categories. Among them are revolution (used in a specific sense), demonstration, terror, dictator-ship, clashes, fall (of a government), demand, claim, order, decision, session, treaty, compromise, agreement, power, property, vote, tax, customs border, wages, unity, freedom, periodicity, situation, relationship, and condition.

11. *Other.* This residual category contains all items that cannot be classi-fied into other categories.

Many terms taken out of their context proved to be ambiguous. Hence, categorization had to be done with the context in mind. Particu-larly problematic was a number of terms that lay between category 5 (social groups with indeterminate membership) and category 8 (abstract forces of history): counter-revolutionary forces, reaction and reform, public opinion, Ultramontane Catholicism (in the sense of a specific tendency in German Catholicism). Separate decisions were made for each occurrence of such terms, in line with the principles outlined above.

Processing the Data. Although in principle the type of data gathered could have been analyzed in its raw form, transferring it to IBM punchcards enabled its rapid analysis using simple tabulating equipment (a counter-sorter). The following codebook was used for coding the data onto the punchcards:

CODEBOOK

Column	Row	
I		*Book*
	0	Neubauer (1903)
	1	Neubauer (1922)
	2	Schnabel (1928)
	3	Gehl (1940)
	4	West Berlin (1966)
	5	East Berlin (1966)
2–4		*Identification Number:* action-oriented assertions are numbered from 001 to 999, by book
5		*Type of Action-Oriented Assertion*
	0	Action sentence
	1	Attributive sentence
	2	Indirect object sentence
	3	Other
6		*Specification of Subject*
	0	Subject specified
	1	Subject not specified (supplied from context or listed as "unknown")
7		*Subject*
	X	Individual: official representative
	0	Individual: private person

Column Row

	1	Social group: membership organization
	2	Social group: nationality or subnationality
	3	Social group: indeterminate membership
	4	Nation-state, city, or other territorial unit
	5	Political institution
	6	Abstract forces of history
	7	Impersonal objects or events
	8	Political objects or events
	9	Other

8

Specification of Object

	0	Object of action specified
	1	Object of action not specified (supplied from context or listed as "unknown")
	2	No object of action

9

Object of Action

	X	Individual: official representative
	0	Individual: private person
	1	Social group: membership organization
	2	Social group: nationality or subnationality
	3	Social group: indeterminate membership
	4	Nation-state, city, or other territorial unit
	5	Political institution
	6	Abstract forces of history
	7	Impersonal objects or events
	8	Political objects or events
	9	Other

10

Aspect of Event Covered

	0	Causes of the Revolution
	1	Revolution in Germany
	2	Revolution in Austria
	3	Revolution in France
	4	Nationalities struggle (Hungary, Italy, Schleswig, Poland)

Column	Row	
	5	Constitutional questions (Paulskirche)
	6	Marx and Engels
11		*Specification of Subject:* insert asterisk *only* if subject is unspecified but can reasonably be presumed
12–45		*Subject:* name written out
46		*Specification of Object of Action:* insert as asterisk *only* if subject is unspecified but can reasonably be presumed
47–80		*Object of Action:* name written out

Before leaving this methodological section I should say a word about controlling for the quality of the data. Ideally, at least two coders should have read the original material, reconstituted the texts into action-oriented assertions, and coded the data. This would have permitted systematic tests to check for consistency and coder reliability, as well as, more generally, the extent to which the coding instructions are understandable and applicable. This multiple-coding procedure was not followed. A desire to concentrate at this stage on determining the overall usefulness of the method, rather than spending time trying to perfect an instrument that may not work out in the long run anyway, meant that we omitted such systematic tests for quality control. The three of us working on the project met frequently, however, to discuss the procedure and to resolve problems that arose. By keeping a careful record of our methodological decisions we sought to ensure consistency. The fact that a single person did all the coding within a space of less than two weeks, and that he had participated in deciding about the specifics of the research design, increased this consistency—but, it must be added, it also increased the possibility of systematic error at one stage or another in the data-gathering process. Further application of the method would demand greater attention to this crucial problem of controlling for the quality of the data.

Perceptions of Participants in the 1848 Revolution

Several aspects of the data presented possibilities for analysis of the images of German textbook writers. Of these, this paper will concentrate upon the general focus of attention of the various texts, differing perceptions of who had participated in the events of the revolution, and the question of interaction among participants.

The Focus of Attention: Developing Historiography. An analysis of the amount of space devoted to various aspects of the 1848 Revolution as a whole sets the framework within which the texts discussed actors and action. A total of twenty-two key aspects were delineated: the Schleswig-Holstein question, the street riots in Berlin and elsewhere, the nationalities struggle in the Austro-Hungarian Empire, the *Vorparlament,* and so forth. The total number of lines devoted in each text to each of the events was tabulated, a ranking made (from the most-discussed to the least-discussed topic) for each book, and the nonparametric Spearman rank-order correlation coefficient used to check the degree of association between each pair of texts.[13] If two rankings are identical in all respects, this measure will produce a score of $r_s = +1.00$; if they are diametrically opposed to one another, the score is $r_s = -1.00$; and if the two rankings bear no resemblance whatsoever to each other (a condition of complete randomness), the score will be $r_s = \pm.00$. Table 1 shows the correlation coefficients for each pair of texts (identified by year of publication, with the book used currently in West Berlin labeled "W-66" and that in East Berlin "E-66").

Of the several points that stand out in Table 1, three are of especial interest. First of all, the degree of association among the first five (i.e., non-Marxist) texts is fairly high, with an average correlation coefficient of $r_s = .68$. In eight of the ten pairs, the correlation coefficient is statistically significant at better than the $p = .02$ level, which means that an analyst would get such a finding by chance only one in fifty times, and the remaining two coefficients are statistically significant at the $p = .10$ level (or one in ten by chance). The two topics to which these five books devoted most space were either the meetings of the National Assembly at

Table 1
DISTRIBUTION OF SPACE ON 22 ASPECTS OF THE 1848 REVOLUTION
Spearman Rank-Order Correlation Coefficients

Book	1903	1922	1928	1940	W-66	E-66
1903		+.99*	+.62*	+.62*	+.49†	−.03
1922	+.99*		+.67*	+.65*	+.50†	+.02
1928	+.62*	+.67*		+.88*	+.65*	+.12
1940	+.62*	+.65*	+.88*		+.70*	+.41†
W-66	+.49†	+.50†	+.65*	+.70*		+.21
E-66	−.03	+.02	+.12	+.41†	+.21	
Average	+.54	+.57	+.59	+.65	+.51	+.15

† Significant at the .10 level for a two-tailed test
* Significant at the .02 level for a two-tailed test

St. Paul's Church (23.7 percent) or the events in Prussia (18.4 percent).

Second, among these five texts there is a steady progression in the changing distribution of space. Viewed as a time series, each book resembles its immediate predecessor or successor more than an earlier or later book. The Neubauer book of 1903, for instance, is almost identical with its 1922 version, less similar to the Schnabel (1928) and Gehl (1940) books, and has still less in common with the West Berlin text of 1966. In turn, the West Berlin text is least like the earlier Neubauer book, and closer to that written under Nazism than to that of the Weimar era. Insofar as focus of attention implies an evaluation of what is important about an event, this finding points to a developing reevaluation of the 1848 Revolution in German historiography—one that continued rather steadily despite changes in official political philosophy. It is a development that may deserve greater examination from a substantive point of view.

Third, the East Berlin text of 1966 is outside the framework of traditional German historiography. Its relationship with four of the other books is not much better than random, and only with Gehl's book (1940) is there any kind of statistically significant correlation. A glance at the data behind the rankings, however, indicates that even this relationship is shaped more by its negative than its positive aspects: both books tend to ignore pretty much the same things. The East Berlin book is much more

Table 2

Book	Number of Persons Mentioned	Number of Lines*	Persons per Line
1903	50	293	.171
1922	52	241	.216
1928	33	436	.071
1940	17	259	.066
W-66	40	705	.058
E-66	29	600	.048

* Standardized to 60-character lines

given over to interpretive sections than are the others, and not surprisingly, it is the only book to pay serious attention to the activities of Marx and Engels during the Revolution (12.2 percent of the total lineage). Fit into a time-series (by ignoring the West Berlin text), it nonetheless conforms to the developing pattern of historiography outlined in the previous paragraph.

The Congruence of Casts of Characters. Turning to the actors themselves, it appears that emphasis upon individual participants has dropped markedly over time, both in terms of the absolute numbers of persons mentioned and relative to the amount of space devoted in the texts to the 1848 Revolution (Table 2). Neubauer's discussions listed 50 and 52 persons as participants in one way or another. Given the relative shortness of his presentations, this means that a new actor appeared on the average of every fifth line. In modern East and West Germany, the number of individual participants declined as the amount of space devoted to the 1848 Revolution rose. The reader of these texts encounters a new personage roughly every twentieth line.

What appears to be a steady change, however, breaks up when we look at the extent to which the texts agreed with one another in their choice of actors. Table 3 uses a simple percentage-agreement index

Table 3

PERCENTAGE AGREEMENT ON PARTICIPANTS BY PAIRS OF BOOKS

Book	1903	1922	1928	1940	W-66	E-66
1903		92%	60%	42%	58%	30%
1922	92%		61	43	59	32
1928	60	61		64	74	42
1940	42	43	64		46	39
W-66	58	59	74	46		35
E-66	30	32	42	39	35	
Average	56%	57%	60%	47%	54%	36%

$$PA = \frac{2ab}{a + b}$$

(where *a* are those names listed in text A, *b* are those listed in text B, and *ab* are those mentioned in both) to show the degree of congruence among the texts. The most congruent pairs are the two Neubauer volumes ($PA = 92$ percent) and the Schnabel (1928) and West Berlin texts ($PA = 74$ percent). Among these four texts, the average percentage-agreement score is $PA = 67$ percent. Between them and the Gehl book of the Nazi era, the congruence is almost a third less ($PA = 49$ percent), and it is only half as great ($PA = 35$ percent) between the four "bourgeois" texts and the East Berlin volume. Again the East Berlin text is the outsider, but two other trends are equally evident. First, the Nazi text also tends to be outside the framework of traditional German historiography, and second, there appears to be an affinity between the texts of Weimar Germany and modern West Berlin.

The Aggregate of Actors. Considering all mentions of all actors (persons, groups, institutions, etc.) produces somewhat the same result. The total number of participants mentioned either as subjects or objects of action were classified into the eleven categories listed in an earlier section of this paper (Table 4). The relative smallness of some of the entries—particularly abstractions (forces of history) but also, somewhat unexpectedly, persons not acting as representatives of their governments—suggested that for further analysis it would be useful to group the data into

Table 4

DISTRIBUTION OF ACTORS (INITIATORS AND OBJECTS OF ACTION)

A. Ungrouped Data

Actor	1903	1922	Book 1928	1940	W-66	E-66
1. Individual: Official	12.4%	12.1%	11.5%	8.5%	9.4%	2.7%
2. Individual: Private	4.9	5.0	2.8	.9	3.5	5.3
3. Group: Membership	2.5	2.0	1.8	4.3	3.0	3.7
4. Group: Nationality	2.1	1.7	3.6	4.4	3.6	1.7
5. Group: Indeterminate	8.3	8.1	12.4	6.6	13.1	30.9
6. Nation-state, City	10.8	12.7	7.5	19.3	9.3	2.6
7. Political Institution	26.3	28.1	23.0	21.8	21.4	17.0
8. Abstract Forces of History	.5	—	1.1	1.2	1.9	1.5
9. Impersonal Events	6.4	3.6	4.7	5.0	8.0	10.4
10. Political Events	23.3	25.7	30.4	25.1	25.8	23.7
11. Other	2.5	1.2	1.2	2.8	.8	.5
Total	100.0	100.2	100.0	99.9	99.8	100.0
N =	760	663	934	742	1,316	1,495

B. Grouped Data

	1903	1922	1928	1940	W-66	E-66
1. Groups (3 + 4 + 5)	12.9%	11.8%	17.8%	15.3%	19.7%	36.3%
2. Institutions (1 + 6 + 7)	49.5	52.9	42.0	49.6	40.1	22.3
3. Political Events (8 + 10)	23.8	25.7	31.5	26.3	27.7	25.2
4. Other (2 + 9 + 11)	13.8	9.8	8.7	8.7	12.3	16.2
Total	100.0	100.2	100.0	99.9	99.8	100.0

four more inclusive categories: groups, political institutions, political events, and a residual category.

As may be seen in Table 5, again the "bourgeois" books—the two by Neubauer, Schnabel's text written in the Weimar Republic, and that used currently in West Berlin—are quite similar (average $r_s = +.93$). Indeed, the latter two differ only in their relative emphasis upon the two smallest categories listed in Table 4. Gehl's text of 1940 tends to diverge somewhat from this high degree of congruence (average $r_s = .88$), more from the Neubauer volumes than from either of those nearest to it in the time-series. And the East Berlin text varied sharply (average $r_s = +.68$). As with the data reported in the previous section, the fact that both the Nazi and East Berlin texts diverge most from the others does not mean that they are near to one another. In this case the correlation coefficient ($r_s = +.53$) for these two books is the lowest shown in Table 5.

Table 5

CONGRUENCE ON THE DISTRIBUTION OF ACTORS

Spearman Rank-Order Correlation Coefficients*

Book	1903	1922	1928	1940	W-66	E-66
1903		+.97	+.91	+.86	+.88	+.66
1922	+.97		+.91	+.85	+.90	+.68
1928	+.91	+.91		+.91	+.99	+.76
1940	+.86	+.85	+.91		+.90	+.53
W-66	+.88	+.90	+.99	+.90		+.77
E-66	+.66	+.68	+.76	+.53	+.77	
Average	+.86	+.86	+.90	+.81	+.89	+.68

* All entries are significant at the .05 level for a two-tailed test

Divergence from the Norm. Another way of viewing these data is in terms of their deviation from the "norm" of German historiography. To get such a baseline, I computed the mean or average percentage of space that the four books from the 1903–1940 period devoted to each of the four categories of grouped data shown in Table 4. The average percentage of references focusing on groups, for instance, is 14.45 percent. A simple statistic (standard deviation) provides an estimate, based upon the data, of the expected variation around the mean for any single observation. Thus, if we assume that the four books included in this survey are truly representative of all history texts published in Germany between 1903 and 1940, and if we select at random another example from this larger class of textbooks, then we would expect the category "groups" to comprise 14.45 ± 2.31 percent (or between 12.14 and 16.76 percent) of the list of actors mentioned in this newly selected book.

The use of standard deviation units reveals the extent to which the West and East Berlin texts vary from what preceded them. As was seen in Table 4, 19.7 percent of the actors listed in the West Berlin text were groups. The difference between this figure and the mean for the four books of the 1903–1940 period ($19.70 - 14.45 = +5.25$) is roughly 2.3 times as great as the standard deviation (Table 6). The share of groups in the East Berlin text diverges from the norm by about 9.5 standard

Table 6

DEVIATION FROM THE 1903–1940 NORM OF WEST AND EAST BERLIN TEXTS

	1903–1940 Norm		*West Berlin Text*			*East Berlin Text*		
Actor	Mean for 1903–1940 $(\bar{X})$	Standard Deviation (s)	Observed Value (X)	Diff. from Mean $(X-\bar{X})$	Std. Dev. Units $\left[\dfrac{X-\bar{X}}{s}\right]$	Observed Value (X)	Diff. from Mean $(X-\bar{X})$	Std. Dev. Units $\left[\dfrac{X-\bar{X}}{s}\right]$
Groups	14.45%	2.31	19.7%	+5.25	+2.27	36.3%	+21.85	+9.46
Inst.	48.50	3.99	40.1	−8.40	−2.11	22.3	−26.20	−6.57
Events	26.83	2.85	27.7	+ .87	+ .31	25.2	− 1.63	− .57
Other	10.25	2.10	12.3	+2.05	+ .98	16.2	+ 5.95	+2.83
Average					±1.42			±4.86

deviation units. The direction of change is the same in both cases: the West and East Berlin texts both pay more attention to groups than we might expect, using as our baseline texts from 1903 to 1940. More interesting is the magnitude of this change. The East Berlin text deviates from the norm by a factor more than four times as great as that characterizing the West Berlin text's divergence. Almost the same is true, in reverse, of attention to political institutions (governments, individuals acting as state representatives, and territorial units such as states) as actors. For the four categories as a whole, the average East Berlin deviation from the 1903–1940 norm is 3.4 times as great as the West Berlin deviation.

Perceptions of Interaction. The question of "who-whom" was a key one in the original research design. What types of action-initiators affected

Table 7

MODEL OF AN INTERACTION MATRIX

Action-Object

γ $\qquad$ δ

		γ	δ
	α	1,1	1,2
Action-Initiator			
	β	2,1	2,2

what types of action-objects? The best way to visualize these relationships is through interaction matrices, as shown schematically in Table 7. The rows in the matrix represent actors (α and β), the columns those acted upon (γ and δ). Hence, if α acts upon δ, then the interaction would be recorded in the first row and the second column (for which the notation is 1,2). Similarly, if β acts upon γ, then the interaction would be recorded in row two, column one (2,1).

Constructing interaction matrices for the textbooks' perceptions of the 1848 Revolution necessitated three preparatory steps. First of all, I eliminated from consideration those assertions that did not involve direct action: attributive sentences, indirect-object sentences, and others not having a subject-object relationship. Second, to get a baseline against which to compare patterns of perceived interaction in the West and East Berlin textbooks, I computed mean scores for the four books published between 1903 and 1940 (as in the previous section). Third, for ease of comparison, I standardized each set of data by transforming them into percentages; hence the sum of all the entries in each matrix (the value of the matrix) is equal to 100.

The first three matrices in Table 8 show the images of interaction in the texts of the 1903–1940 period, of West Berlin, and of East Berlin. Matrix D shows the difference between the West Berlin matrix and that of the baseline period (B–A), Matrix E the difference between the East Berlin and the baseline matrix (C–A), and Matrix F the difference between the West Berlin and East Berlin matrices (C–B).

Table 8
MATRICES OF INTERACTION

A. 1903–40 Norm: Basic Data

	Grp	Ins	Evt	Oth	Tot
Grp	2	9	6	1	18
Ins	5	27	20	3	55
Evt	1	5	8	2	16
Oth	2	4	3	2	11
Tot	10	45	37	8	100

B. West Berlin: Basic Data

	Grp	Ins	Evt	Oth	Tot
Grp	3	8	11	3	25
Ins	6	21	17	4	48
Evt	3	4	8	2	17
Oth	1	3	2	4	10
Tot	13	36	38	13	100

C. East Berlin: Basic Data

	Grp	Ins	Evt	Oth	Tot
Grp	10	9	22	9	50
Ins	8	10	7	3	28
Evt	1	1	6	1	9
Oth	3	1	6	3	13
Tot	22	21	41	16	100

D. W. Bln: Change from Norm

	Grp	Ins	Evt	Oth	Tot
Grp	+1	−1	+5	+2	+7
Ins	+1	−6	−3	+1	−7
Evt	+2	−1	±0	±0	+1
Oth	−1	−1	−1	+2	−1
Tot	+3	−9	+1	+5	±0

E. E. Bln: Change from Norm

	Grp	Ins	Evt	Oth	Tot
Grp	+8	±0	+16	+8	+32
Ins	+3	−17	−13	±0	−27
Evt	±0	−4	−2	−1	−7
Oth	+1	−3	+3	+1	+2
Tot	+12	−24	+4	+8	±0

F. Diff.: East and West Bln

	Grp	Ins	Evt	Oth	Tot
Grp	+7	+1	+11	+6	+25
Ins	+2	−11	−10	−1	−20
Evt	−2	−3	−2	−1	−8
Oth	+2	−2	+4	−1	+3
Tot	+9	−15	+3	+3	±0

A first glance at the matrices of change for the West Berlin (D) and East Berlin (E) texts confirms the finding noted in the previous section. The cumulative changes (row-totals and column-totals) show that both moved toward a greater emphasis on groups and away from a primary concern with institutional actors. Moreover, the East Berlin text moved much more sharply in both directions than did that used in the classrooms of West Berlin. The average cell entry in the East Berlin matrix of change (E), that is, the average amount of change from the 1903–1940 norm, was ±5.0, almost three times as great as the average cell entry in the West Berlin matrix of change (±1.8).

Closer examination reveals interesting shifts in the perception of interaction. For the West Berlin matrix of change (D), the greatest single shift was reduced attention to institutions acting upon institutions ($2,2 = -6$). Even so, referring back to the basic data matrix for West Berlin (B), this cell entry remains the largest of all, as during the 1903–1940 baseline period (A) as well. The only other change worth noting is increased attention to groups acting upon or producing events ($1,3 = +5$). This shift accounts for most of the West Berlin book's increased emphasis upon groups as actors. It nonetheless remains a poor third to institutions affecting either other institutions (Matrix B, $2,2 = 21$) or producing events (Matrix B, $2,3 = 17$). For West Berlin's textbook writers, group interaction (Matrix B, $1,1 = 3$) remains quite unimportant.

By comparison, the changed perspectives in East Berlin's book (Matrix E) are striking. Most noticeable is the sharply reduced attention to institutions affecting either other institutions ($2,2 = -17$) or events ($2,3 = -13$). Also significant is the markedly increased attention to groups affecting events ($1,3 = +16$). The average shift of these three cell entries for the East Berlin text is more than three times as great as the average change for the West Berlin text.

One aspect of the data in Matrix E poses an interesting problem for further investigation. Although the East Berlin text differs from the 1903–1940 norm in its perception of groups acting upon other groups ($1,1 = +8$), events ($1,3 = +16$), and other actors ($1,4 = +8$, primarily impersonal objects, by the way), it differs not at all regarding groups affecting institutions ($1,2 = \pm 0$). The finding itself suggests that the Marxist-oriented textbook writers in East Berlin did not see groups (for the most part, according to the raw data, social classes, and more specifically, the working class) as being influential during the 1848 Revolution vis-à-vis the government and its agencies. Is this a finding that is generally valid, or only for the specific event? What would an analysis of a subsequent event reveal—most especially after 1949 when, according to the communist rhetoric, the "First German Workers' and Peasants' State" came into being? An unsystematic reading of the texbook's treatment of the postwar era indicates that the relationship is indeed changed, that social groups are seen to have an extensive impact upon the (East German) state. Without additional information we cannot tell whether the changed imagery is deliberate or unconscious. It would seem, however, that this changed imagery (assuming that this supposition is borne out by additional empirical research) is in line with overt communist doctrine.

Differences between the matrices of change for the West Berlin (D) and East Berlin (E) texts are substantial, as may be seen in Matrix F, and generally along the lines discussed in preceding paragraphs. The average magnitudes of the cells reveal that the West Berlin text is much further away from the East Berlin text (±4.1) than its predecessors (±1.8). There is a smaller difference between the East Berlin text's distance from the 1903–1940 norm (±5.0) and from the West Berlin text (±4.1). Spearman rank-order correlation coefficients (shown in part in Table 9) indicate much the same finding: for West Berlin and the norm (B,A), $r_s = +.83$; for East Berlin and the norm (C,A), $r_s = +.42$; and for West and East Berlin (B,C), $r_s = +.61$. (In the case of the East Berlin text and the norm, the degree of correlation is not significant at the $p = .10$ level for a two-tailed test; in the other two cases, the coefficient is significant at the $p = .02$ level. Phrased more generally, the difference between matrices A and C is statistically significant, whereas those between matrices A and B and matrices B and C are not.)

Looking more carefully at the sources of current images of interaction (Table 9), it again appears that the "bourgeois" texts are more like one

Table 9

INTERCORRELATION OF INTERACTION MATRICES

Book	1903	1922	1928	1940	W-66	E-66
1903		+.87*	+.78*	+.48†	+.85*	+.49†
1922	+.87*		+.75*	+.65*	+.74*	+.21
1928	+.78*	+.75*		+.86*	+.76*	+.45†
1940	+.48†	+.65*	+.86*		+.68*	+.33
W-66	+.85*	+.74*	+.76*	+.68*		+.61*
E-66	+.49†	+.21	+.45†	+.33	+.61*	
Average	+.69	+.64	+.72	+.60	+.73	+.42

† Significant at the .10 level for a two-tailed test
* Significant at the .02 level for a two-tailed test

another (average $r_s = +.79$) than they are like either the Nazi (average $r_s = +.67$) or Marxist (average $r_s = +.44$). But again, as was the case earlier, the East German text is not at all close to the Nazi text by Walther Gehl ($r_s = +.33$).

Conclusions

The findings to emerge from this pilot project are several. The first pertains to the method itself. Although it is clear that the methodology needs refinement—particularly with regard to the reconstitution of the text into action-oriented assertions—it nonetheless appears to be an appropriate way to get at certain types of information. It is flexible. The scholar can adapt it easily to his own purposes, and to several languages. It is inexpensive in research time and resources. The project reported here required 140 hours of coding time and about nine hours to transfer the data (first ten columns only) to punchcards. Finally, it does not require electronic equipment, nor must the analyst possess statistical sophistication or computer skills. It is a do-it-yourself technique. And it is in this light that its output must be viewed.

The cost of simplicity in this case is that the output of information, however useful, is limited. Adding a dimension of affect would be desirable. It would be possible to determine from the context whether the texts view the participants in historical events in a favorable or not so favorable light. It should also be possible to score the predicates or verbs on an active-passive scale. But to add such twists would increase the complexity of the method; and the point might soon be reached at which it would be more efficient to undertake a full-scale computer analysis using a system like the General Inquirer. When the researcher wants merely to get indicators of the direction and magnitude of differentiated perspectives, or of shifts in such perspectives over time, the method is both appropriate and convenient.

The substantive findings of the analysis, although diverse, almost all point in the same direction. (1) The history text currently used in East Berlin's high schools differs significantly in its perspectives from that in use on the western side of the Brandenburg Gate.

(2) The East Berlin text has moved further from traditional German

historiography on the question of the 1848 Revolution than has the West Berlin text. A developmental pattern appears to characterize this historiography; and in some respects both texts clearly are a continuation of this pattern. But the East Berlin book has moved far enough in other respects that it can be described as beyond the pale from a traditional point of view. Available quantitative indicators suggest that the magnitude of the shift made by the East German textbook writers is roughly three times as great as the shift from the 1903–1940 norm made by textbook authors in the West.

(3) Although the text written during the Nazi period also tends to be outside traditional German historiography, it is not similar to the East Berlin text. The proposition that totalitarianisms of both the right and left are basically similar is not supported by data on perspectives vis-à-vis actors in history. Clearly, however, it is possible that in other aspects of history writing they share key attributes, such as, perhaps, a propensity to use descriptive adjectives designed to have an emotional impact upon their readers.

(4) If there is any single text particularly close to that now used in West Berlin, it is the book written by Franz Schnabel during the Weimar era. And yet the statistical data indicate that there is only a suggestion of such a tie. The two books differ in too many regards to say simply that one is the spiritual father of the other. Indeed, the correlation of their interaction matrices reveals that the West Berlin book is closer to that published during the heyday of the Wilhelmine Reich than to that of Weimar Germany! The complexity of the various relationships discussed in this paper denies the proposition that the historical perspectives of Weimar and Bonn or West Berlin are identical.

(5) As far as the substance of postwar changes in historical perspectives is concerned, the relative importance of groups is the crucial factor. The East Berlin text is far more inclined than the West Berlin text to stress groups as initiators of action—except with respect to the state and its agents. This is not to say that the West Berlin text has not moved at all in the direction of emphasis upon groups, but merely that by comparison it is the East Berlin text that is strongly oriented toward the behavior of groups in history.

The sum of these variations means that students in East and West Berlin are currently receiving images of their past that not only differ from one side of the city to the other but, in the East Berlin case at least, differ sharply from traditional German historical scholarship. As pointed out earlier, we have no empirical data to tell us the extent to which other socializing agents (particularly teachers and parents) reinforce or contradict these images. Nor do we know the extent to which students internalize them. It nonetheless seems reasonable to expect that these varying images are contributing their bit to a growing psychic distance between East and West Berliners, between East and West Germans. In this respect it is not merely the contrasting images of participants in the 1848 Revolution that are important (if for no other reason than the fact that this event is not a leading topic of conversation when people meet). What counts is the concept underlying the image—the role in everyday life of human groups versus more or less impersonal institutions—no less than the value of political participation that it implies. In developing a participant society in which individuals united into groups can achieve common ends, or a society in which the individual pursues personal goals in a framework of struggling but impersonal institutions, such a concept is important.

Comment 6

◆

John Higham

DEPARTMENT OF HISTORY, UNIVERSITY OF MICHIGAN

As I UNDERSTAND HIM, Merritt had two general objectives in making a content analysis of German textbooks. We should take careful note of the relative importance his research design assigns to each.

One aim was to discover how much the underlying historical outlook of the German people has changed in the twentieth century. Our attention is especially drawn to the question: how far have East and West Germany diverged in historical outlook, and how far has each of them moved from the historical assumptions that prevailed before World War II? It is not, however, the whole, vast range of assumptions about the past that is in question. Instead, Merritt has asked specifically about the relative importance Germans have assigned to different types of causal agents. To what extent do they remember their own national experience as a product of individual initiative, of group action, and of political institutions?

If this were Merritt's only objective, we might have expected him to examine the standard textbooks in their entirety, consult the scholarly and interpretive works of influential German historians, and perhaps glance at prominent state papers and commemorative addresses to draw out the historical values imbedded there as well. We might have expected him to compare the treatment of various events, quote salient judgments, embellish his account with vivid examples, and offer an overall estimate of the inter-relation of person, group, and institution in the conceptual framework of each book or each era under consideration. Instead, he has restricted himself to an examination of one historical event in just six textbooks. Moreover, he has austerely excluded all concrete detail about the presentation of that event in individual books, preferring to confine himself to statistical abstractions.

Clearly, a second objective explains the strict limits Merritt put on the scope of his research. He wished to make a methodological experiment. He wished to try out a somewhat new technique of content analysis, a technique that his paper explains with admirable clarity and precision. I find myself simultaneously admiring the elegance and apparent economy of his procedures and worrying about the price he has paid for them.

Evidently, the more systematic one's methods become, the smaller is the proportion or the range of data one can handle relative to the universe those data are supposed to represent. Historians, as a group, have culti- vated a skill in dealing with relatively large, miscellaneous aggregations of data. Their work is strong in contextual density, for they want to take account of the multiplicity of phenomena impinging upon or present within the situation under scrutiny. Every step toward the systematization of research, involving as it does the exclusion of data the system cannot handle, poses a special problem for historians. How far can they go in restricting their inputs without experiencing a net loss in the results they attain? There is no easy answer to this question. But it needs to be posed, insistently and repeatedly. We cannot afford the easy assumption so prevalent in some quarters that every addition to a historian's repertory of methods is a net gain. The historian who would make, not the maximum but the most effective, use of various methods must ask how compatible they may be with one another, how much time and energy he should invest in each, and what order of importance he can assign to their respective findings.

Attending strictly to the first of Merritt's two objectives, a historian is likely to wonder if it could not have been more persuasively attained without any formal content analysis at all. No one familiar with the course of modern historiography will wonder that textbooks in *any* western country have become more concerned with groups and less concerned with institutions. The shift from political and institutional history to a social and group-centered approach is, after all, the most obvious single trend in historical writing in the twentieth century.[14] Though exhibited most sweepingly in Marxist historiography, this trend has significantly altered the bourgeois sense of the past as well. We would be entitled to be surprised by Merritt's research only if it showed something else.

To be sure, he has put the matter in terms of a numerical scale; he has given us some tables and boxes that we would not otherwise have. Yet I cannot believe that this mathematical demonstration—subject as it is to all the theoretical criticism Merritt himself knows so well how to make— can be as persuasive as a full qualitative appraisal replete with striking examples and based on a more extensive literature. The systematic method that was employed had the particular disadvantage of excluding from purview so much historical writing as to leave the analyst apparently unaware of the larger currents of historiography within which his selected textbooks had their being.

To leave the matter here would be manifestly unfair. Merritt might correctly reply that the potential value of his method should not be decided on the admittedly tentative and preliminary results of an initial experiment. Conceivably the method could be improved and applied to other countries in ways that might discriminate the specifically German from the generically modern trends in historical consciousness. Merritt's earlier work on American national consciousness has already demonstrated that content analysis can bring to light some aspects of the history of popular thought that might not be discerned without his kind of methodological rigor.[15] Nevertheless this defense, which asks us to give recognition to the possible fruitfulness of a type of inquiry, if it is pushed much further than the author for the moment is prepared to go, points up the importance of Merritt's second objective, and reveals in the paper before us the primacy of method over substance. How shall we judge his methodological proposal, or any other for that matter, without having the results it promises already in hand? How important is discussion of theory, strategy, and tactics anyway? These questions suggest a basic distinction between two styles of scholarship.

In the United States far too much has been made of alleged differences between history and social science. We have conceived of "social science" as a real entity that needs to be differentiated from or (according to one's preference) reconciled with the humanistic studies. In so doing Americans have created a myth of social science and a caricature of history.[16] I propose an alternative dichotomy cutting across all the conventional divisions in the study of man, and I believe it may on the whole yield a better insight into the distinct but complementary roles scholars play. Let us, for the moment at least, think of one type of scholar as devoted chiefly to *process,* while another type is interested primarily in *product.*

The process-oriented scholar enjoys the pursuit of truth more than the possession of it. He revels in methodological debate, in the careful construction of research designs, in the most rigorous criticism of substantive findings. He does not mind at all getting negative results. Indeed, one of the chief values of his work is in disproving bits of conventional wisdom, in showing for example that a colorful incident did not decide a presidential election. Characteristically, he stresses the incompleteness of his own work and regards his publications as interim reports, case studies, theoretical models, or simply as contributions to a continuing cultural dialog. Yet his emphasis on the shortcomings of present knowledge and opinion is generally balanced by expectations of the great advances that lie just ahead as our methods improve.

The product-oriented scholar, on the other hand, cares more about the completeness or the coherence of his work than he does about its replication or extension by others. He is unappreciative of negative findings, intolerant of theoretical claims, and unwilling to risk the waste (for him) of time and effort that may be involved in methodological experimentation. He seeks to construct relatively self-sufficient, relatively finished products. He may be quite pragmatic about methods, quite willing to use a variety of them if they offer efficient, convergent routes to solid results. But his principal aim is never to design a technique or to test a theory. He wants rather to create—however small it may be—a cultural achievement, not to contribute to an ongoing process.

All typologies simplify and in a measure distort. Nobody sacrifices procedure completely to substance or substance wholly to procedure. Preferences are relative; they form a continuum, and some of us fluctuate back and forth a good deal between the two poles. Yet the distinction suggested here has at least the merit of breaking into the conventional dichotomy between historians and social scientists.

It is true that historians, in whatever discipline one finds them, tend to be strongly product-minded. From the point of view of their critics, that makes them methodologically naive, though the naiveté is rooted in skills and sensitivities that do not seem susceptible to systematization. In contrast, most contemporary social scientists, together with many philosophers and some literary critics, are process-minded, which means among other things that they publish lots of articles and collaborative studies but relatively few integrated books, and that they like to evaluate scholarly work more in terms of upcoming trends than in terms of substantial achievement. Nevertheless, some historians—an increasing number at present—are very much process-minded. They have taken upon themselves a special burden and risk. Similarly, some social scientists are chiefly product-minded. They too must resist the predominant ethos in their respective disciplines.

What we have often imagined during the last fifty years to be a problem of the relationship between historian and social scientist might better be understood as a difference between two styles of scholarship, both of which reach into all disciplines, though in varying proportions. Both are valuable, though neither can be fairly judged by the criteria of the other. In spite of the frequent claims of the process-minded, neither style is necessarily more scientific than the other, for each defines science in its own way: one sees it as a method of inquiry; the other considers it a body of knowledge. A wider appreciation of these differences cannot and probably should not resolve them. But such appreciation can bring a clearer perception of the dilemmas posed by conferences and symposia of the kind we are attending.

Notes

Public Opinion Quarterly is sometimes cited as *POQ.*

Chapter 1—Small and Singer

I am indebted to Athan Theoharis of Marquette University and Ronald P. Formisano of the University of Rochester for their aid with this paper (M. S.).

1. *Public Opinion* (New York 1961 [1922]): 253.
2. Joseph Strayer writes, "Historians have been talking about the importance of public opinion longer perhaps than any other professional group." "The Historian's Concept of Public Opinion," ed. Mirra Komarovsky, *Common Frontiers of the Social Sciences* (Glencoe 1957): 263.
3. Portions of this paper have appeared in "The American Image of Germany, 1906–1914" (Ph.D. diss., University of Michigan, 1965).
4. Walter Lippmann sees World War I as the demarcation point after which all governments were forced to truckle emotionally to their publics. *Essays in the Public Philosophy* (Boston 1955).
5. See Paul F. Lazarsfeld, "The Historian and the Pollster," ed. Komarovsky [n. 2]: 242–62.
6. An examination of course offerings in history departments of American universities demonstrates the disproportionate interest in the years since the French Revolution.
7. See William L. Langer's presidential address to the American Historical Association, "The Next Assignment," *American Historical Review* 63 (Jan. 1958): 283–304.
8. Snyder and Furniss, *American Foreign Policy Formulation* (New York 1954): 523; Perkins, "The Department of State and American Public Opinion," ed. Gordon A. Craig and Felix Gilbert, *The Diplomats,* 1 (New York 1965 [1953]): 283; U.S. Dept. of State, *American Public Opinion and Foreign Policy,* Pub. 6925 (Washington 1960): 2. See also Bernadotte Schmitt, "The Relation Between Public Opinion and Foreign Affairs Before and During the First World War," ed. Arshag O. Sarkissian, *Studies in Diplomatic History and Historiography* (London 1961): 321–30; Richard R. Fagen, "Some Assessments and Uses of Public Opinion in Diplomacy," *POQ* 24 (Fall 1960): 448–57; Milton J. Rosenberg, "Images in Relation to the Policy Process," ed. Herbert C. Kelman, *International Behavior* (New York 1965): 285.
9. Gabriel A. Almond sees the public as setting "certain criteria in the form of widely held values and expectations," while James M. Rosenau talks of "citizens comprising the mass public who *limit* the range of acceptable alternatives" for policy makers. Almond, *The American People and Foreign Policy* (New York 1961 [1950]): 5; Rosenau, *National Leadership and Foreign Policy* (Princeton 1963): 3. See also Strayer [n. 2]: 266.
10. For a discussion of presidential control of opinion, see James Reston, *The Artillery of the Press* (New York 1967): 48–50.

11. An invaluable source which surveys the important studies in the field is Joseph T. Klapper, *The Effects of Mass Communication* (New York 1960). Another useful introduction, with extensive bibliography, is Carl I. Hovland, "Effects of Mass Media of Communication," ed. Gardner Lindzey, *Handbook of Social Psychology*, 2 (Reading, Mass., 1954): 1062–103. For a bibliographic treatment by a historian, see Ernest R. May, "An American Tradition in Foreign Policy: The Role of Public Opinion," ed. William H. Nelson, *Theory and Practice in American Politics* (Chicago 1964): 101–22.

12. In her preface to a study of textbooks, Ruth M. Elson writes: "To discover what ideas were held by the ordinary man in any period of history is one of the persistent problems of intellectual history. The ideas and ideological development of literary men can be analyzed . . . But the ordinary man, unliterary by nature, left no direct expression of the concepts he accepted. His household furniture and artifacts offer source material for social history, but his intellectual furniture rarely appears in a form capable of surviving him. What the averbal man of the past thought about anything is probably lost forever to historical research, but one can at least discover those ideas to which most Americans were exposed by examining the books they read." *Guardians of Tradition: American Schoolbooks of the Nineteenth Century* (Lincoln 1964): iv.

13. For the development of the historical study of public opinion, see Paul F. Lazarsfeld, "Public Opinion and the Classical Tradition," ed. Charles S. Steinberg, *Mass Media and Communication* (New York 1966): 79–111.

14. Hazen explains that he wants "to show from the writings of the men of that time what that opinion was." *Contemporary American Opinion of the French Revolution* (Baltimore 1897): x. Typical Hazen products are John G. Gazley, *American Opinion of German Unification* (New York 1926); Miriam B. Urban, *British Opinion and Policy on the Unification of Italy, 1856–61* (Scottdale, Pa., 1938).

15. (Cambridge, Mass., 1941): vi, 38.

16. *French Public Opinion and Foreign Affairs, 1870–1914* (New York 1931): vii. See also idem, *Germany and the Great Powers, 1866–1914* (New York 1938).

17. Idem, *French Public Opinion*: 8.

18. *Ibid.*: 23. Italics mine.

19. Winston B. Thorson, "American Public Opinion and the Portsmouth Peace Conference," *American Historical Review* 53 (Apr. 1948): 444, 454.

20. Eleanor Tupper and George E. McReynolds, *Japan in American Public Opinion* (New York 1937): 35. On occasion they do qualify their statements, e.g., "American public opinion as seen in newspapers and periodicals" (445).

21. *A Diplomatic History of the American People* (New York 1964): 671, 391. See also idem, *Man in the Street* (New York 1948). The striking gulf between two related cultures is seen when this book is compared to Almond's [n. 9], which appeared only two years later. For other transgressors, see Kingsley Martin, *The Triumph of Lord Palmerston* (London 1963 [1924]); Frederick Merk, *Manifest Destiny and Mission in American History* (New York 1966): 35–39; Foster R. Dulles, *America's Rise to World Power, 1898–1954* (New York 1955); Raymond Postgate and Aylmer Vallance, *England Goes to Press* (Indianapolis 1937): 83; Lynn M. Case, *French Opinion on the United States and Mexico* (New York 1936); vii–xi. In the last work Case warns against using editorials, but two decades later he reverts to their use, although "sparingly and with caution." *French Opinion on War and Diplomacy During the Second Empire* (Philadelphia 1954): 6.

22. (Washington 1941): 163–64.

23. "Toward a Science of Public Opinion," *POQ* 1 (Jan. 1937): 10. See also Lucy M. Solomon, *The Newspaper and the Historian* (New York 1923): 252, 470–71.

24. Wilson, "The Press and Public Opinion in Erie County, Ohio," *Journalism Quarterly* 18 (Mar. 1944): 14–17; Mott, "Newspapers in Presidential Campaigns," *POQ* 8 (Fall 1944): 348–67; Lundberg, "The Newspaper and Public Opinion," *Social Forces* 4 (June 1926): 709–15. For a discussion of the relationship between newspapers and opinion from a different perspective, see Julian L. Woodward, "Quantitative News Analysis as a Technique of Opinion Research," *ibid.* 12 (May 1934), 526–37.

25. *Public Opinion and American Democracy* (New York 1961): 351, 353. The average reader probably reads from a tenth to a third of the news content of a paper. Wilbur Schramm, "Measuring Another Dimension of Newspaper Readership," *Journalism Quarterly* 24 (Dec. 1947): 295. See also Charles E. Swanson, "What They Read in 130 Daily Newspapers," *ibid.* 32 (Fall 1955): 411–21. Among those who report a greater interest in editorials than commonly expected are James C. MacDonald, "Newspaper Editorial Readership and Length of Editorials," *ibid.* 38 (Autumn 1961): 473–79; Wilbur Schramm and David White, "Age, Education, Economic Status: Factors in Newspaper Reading," *ibid.* 26 (June 1949): 149–59.

26. William Albig, *Public Opinion* (New York 1939): 404–6.

27. See Reston [n. 10]: 63.

28. *Americans in World Affairs* (Boston 1959): 9–10. Almond assails the "typical indifference [of Americans] to foreign policy in the absence of threat" ([n. 9]: 86). James Rosenau finds indifference to foreign affairs common in from 75 to 90 percent of the population. *Public Opinion and Foreign Policy* (New York 1961): 35–36. See also Martin Kriesberg, "Dark Areas of Ignorance," ed. Lester Markel, *Public Opinion and Foreign Policy* (New York 1949): 51.

29. I am indebted to Gerald K. Haines for information in this area.

30. To Annie Grew (his mother), Sept. 13, 1912, Joseph C. Grew papers, Harvard University. This outburst was precipitated by the discovery of an article on the death of the Japanese emperor tucked away on p. 3 of the *Washington Post.* Ten leading American papers in 1910 devoted around 3 percent of their non-advertising copy to foreign news. Frank L. Mott, "Trends in Newspaper Content," *Annals* 219 (Jan. 1942): 61. A good if somewhat outdated bibliography is in Ralph O. Nafziger, *International News and the Press* (New York 1940).

31. Carroll, *French Public Opinion* [n. 16]: *passim;* Cohen, *The Press and Foreign Policy* (Princeton 1963): 234–36. Cohen does point out that editorials are watched more for negative than positive expressions of opinion. A demonstration of diplomatic interest in editorials does not necessarily prove policies were affected by them. See the difficulty Oron J. Hale has in *Publicity and Diplomacy* (New York 1940): 39–40 and *passim.* Of course, editorials often affect diplomats in other countries. *Ibid.:* 293. One officer of the U.S. State Dept. told Markel, "We read the digests, we ponder the polls, and then we are likely to be influenced by our favorite columnist." "Opinion—A Neglected Instrument," ed. Markel [n. 28]: 31.

32. [n. 31]: 13.

33. Horace C. Peterson, *Propaganda for War* (Norman 1939): 7; Angus Campbell and Charles A. Metzner, "Books, Libraries and Other Media of Communication," ed. Daniel Katz et al., *Public Opinion and Propaganda* (New York 1964): 235–42. For more recent periods it is likely television has replaced all other media as the prime influence on the public.

See Reston [n. 10]: 50. For the relationship between newspaper, book, and magazine readership and an informed public, see Ralph O. Nafziger et al., "The Mass Media and an Informed Public," *POQ* 15 (Spring 1951): 105–13.

34. Martin [n. 21]: 22–23.

35. Carl I. Hovland, Irving L. Janis, and Harold H. Kelley, *Communication and Persuasion* (New Haven 1953): 6; Leonard Doob, *Public Opinion and Propaganda* (New York 1948): 36; Albig [n. 26]: 1. See also Harwood L. Childs, *An Introduction to Public Opinion* (New York 1949).

36. "Attitudes" has been ignored explicitly because, of the three terms, it is the most unclear.

37. Kenneth Boulding, *The Image* (Ann Arbor 1956): 5; Richard Fagen, *Politics and Communication* (Boston 1966): 7; Lippmann [n. 1]: 3. Unfortunately, the use of the term today brands one as a faddist. Among the scores of recent "image" studies are Cushing Strout, *The American Image of the Old World* (New York 1963); Merrill D. Peterson, *The Jefferson Image in the American Mind* (New York 1960); Ernest R. May (ed.), *The American Image Series,* 4 v. (New York 1963); Philip D. Curtin, *The Image of Africa* (Madison 1964); Daniel J. Boorstin, *America and the Image of Europe* (New York 1960), *The Image: Or What Happened to the American Dream* (New York 1961); Franklin K. Kilpatrick, Milton C. Cummings, and M. Kent Jennings, *The Image of the Federal Service* (Washington 1964); Raymond L. Bruckberger, *Images of America* (New York 1959), originally pub. in France as *La République Américaine* (1958). Few of these authors do anything about defining "image."

38. Ithiel de Sola Pool and Kali Prasad, "Indian Student Images of Foreign People," *POQ* 22 (Fall 1958): 292–93.

39. Lippmann [n. 1]: 68.

40. "Switzerland" in headlines would probably elicit the same types of responses that Harold Isaacs receives when he asks Americans what first comes into their minds when he mentions "China." "Scratches on Our Minds," *POQ* 20 (Spring 1956): 198. This earlier article discusses problems involved in *Scratches on Our Minds* (Cambridge, Mass., 1958).

41. 5: *Over Here, 1914–1918* (New York 1933): 53–56.

42. Martin [n. 21]: 20.

43. Lee Benson would of course add voting and demographic statistics, but these are more relevant in domestic politics. "An Approach to the Scientific Study of Past Public Opinion," *POQ* 31 (Winter 1967–68): 522–67.

44. Much of the work for 19th century America has been done by Elson [n. 12].

45. James W. Gerard, *Face to Face with Kaiserism* (New York 1918): 283.

46. See for example, John T. Flanagan, "The German in American Fiction," ed. Oscar F. Ander, *In the Trek of the Immigrants* (Rock Island 1964): 95–113.

47. An example of a broader analysis of intellectual climate is Norbert J. Grossman, "Political and Social Themes in the English Popular Novel, 1815–1832," *POQ* 20 (Fall 1956): 531–41.

48. I am indebted to Larry Powe and James Garrett, who read these 16 novels word by word. Originally we planned to read and code the top 10 novels from each year's best seller list for the period 1906–14, but after examining 16, we decided the effort was hardly worth it. For best seller lists, see *Bookman;* Alice P. Hackett, *60 Years of Best Sellers, 1895–1955* (New York 1956); Frank L. Mott, *Golden Multitudes* (New York 1947). One should bear in mind that even present day lists are far from accurate. Boorstin, *The Image* [n. 37]: 165–66.

49. Books about international relations were found to be among the most popular with all classes of readers in the late 1920s. Douglas Waples and Ralph W. Tyler, *What People Want to Read About* (Chicago 1931): 70.

50. Paul F. Lazarsfeld, Bernard Berelson, and Hazel Gaudet, *The People's Choice* (New York 1960): 135–36. The historian can only wish he had studies for his particular epoch like Lazarsfeld and Rowena Wyatt, "Magazines in Twenty Cities: Who Reads What?" *POQ* 1 (Oct. 1937): 29–41.

51. See Bernard Berelson and Patricia J. Salter, "Majority and Minority Americans; an Analysis of Magazine Fiction," *POQ* 10 (Summer 1946): 168–90.

52. Some argue that people tend to select reading material which conforms to their preconceived images. Charles F. Cannell and James C. MacDonald, "The Impact of Health News on Attitudes and Behavior," *Journalism Quarterly* 33 (Summer 1956): 315–23.

53. Walter Lippmann says, "Pictures have always been the surest way of conveying an idea" ([n. 1]: 162).

54. For an introduction to content analysis see Robert C. North et al., *Content Analysis* (Evanston 1963); Richard L. Merritt, "The Representational Model in Cross-National Content-Analysis," ed. Joseph L. Bernd, *Mathematical Applications in Political Science*, 2 (Dallas 1966): 44–71; idem, "Public Opinion in Colonial America; Content Analyzing the Colonial Press," *POQ* 37 (Fall 1963): 356–71.

55. Pool et al., *The Prestige Papers* (Stanford 1952); Pool, *Symbols of Internationalism* (Stanford 1951).

56. *Symbols of American Community, 1735–1775* (New Haven 1966).

57. Useful here are Milton D. Stewart, "Importance in Content Analysis," *Journalism Quarterly* 20 (Dec. 1943): 286–93; Ralph O. Nafziger, "The Reading Audience," ed. Wilbur Schramm, *Communications in Modern Society* (Urbana 1948): 102–15. For some of the problems of discrimination between materials, see Percy H. Tannenbaum, "The Effects of Headlines on the Interpretation of News Stories," *Journalism Quarterly* 30 (Spring 1953): 189–97; Reuben Mehling, "Attitude Changing Effect of News and Photo Combinations," *ibid.* 36 (Spring 1959): 189–98.

58. The enormity of the task might be eased by a computer, but the computer is still only as good as the man-made coding rules. See Philip J. Stone et al., *The General Inquirer* (Cambridge, Mass., 1966).

59. For the classic presentation of the theory, see Katz and Lazarsfeld, *Personal Influence* (Glencoe 1955). See also Katz, "The Two Step Flow of Communication," ed. Wilbur Schramm, *Mass Communication* (Urbana 1960): 346–65; Stanley K. Bigman, "Prestige, Personal Influence, and Opinion," ed. Wilbur Schramm, *The Process and Effects of Mass Communication* (Urbana 1961): 402–10; Kenneth P. Adler and Davis Bobrow, "Interest and Influence in Foreign Affairs," *POQ* 20 (Spring 1956): 89–101. A recent study by a historian makes use of the personal influence model: Ernest R. May, *American Imperialism* (New York 1968).

60. "The Nature of Belief Systems in Mass Publics," ed. David Apter, *Ideology and Discontent* (New York 1964): 206–61.

61. Raymond A. and Alice Bauer, "America, 'Mass Society' and Mass Media," ed. Steinberg [n. 13]: 445–46.

62. Hovland et al. [n. 35]: 23; Percy H. Tannenbaum, "Initial Attitudes Toward Source as Factors in Attitude Change Through Mass Communication," *POQ* 20 (Summer 1956): 413–25.

63. Hovland et al. [n. 35]: 254.

64. Karl Deutsch and Richard L. Merritt, "Effects of Events on National and International Images," ed. Kelman [n. 8]: 182.

65. Almond [n. 9]: 69–115.

66. The optimum solution would be a study like William Buchanan and Hadley Cantril, *How Nations See Each Other* (Urbana 1953).

67. Carl I. Hovland, "Reconciling Conflicting Results Derived from Experimental and Survey Studies of Attitude Change," ed. E. P. Hollander and Raymond G. Hunt, *Current Perspectives in Social Psychology* (New York 1963): 378–89.

Chapter 2—Lazarsfeld and Perkins

1. "Attitude: The History of a Concept," *Perspectives in American History*, 1 (1967): 287 ff.

2. *Essays on Politics and History*, 1 (Berlin 1914): 203–4.

3. Paul F. Lazarsfeld et al., *The People's Choice*, 3rd ed. (New York 1968); Key, *Politics, Parties and Pressure Groups* (New York 1942); Free and Cantril, *The Political Beliefs of Americans* (New Brunswick 1967).

4. *The Achieving Society* (Princeton 1961).

5. "Need for Achievement and English Industrial Growth," *Economic Development and Cultural Change* 10 (Oct. 1961): 8–20, 19 (graph).

6. "Machiavelli," *Critical and Historical Essays*, 2 (London 1919): 14–15. Italics mine.

7. The study was carried on by J. G. Blumer and D. McQuail at the University of Leeds.

8. "Research Problems in American Historiography," ed. Mirra Komarovsky, *Common Frontiers of the Social Sciences* (Glencoe 1957): 113–82.

9. *The Concept of Jacksonian Democracy* (Princeton 1961).

10. William N. McPhee and William Glaser (eds.) *Public Opinion in Congressional Elections* (New York 1962).

11. "Relational Analysis: The Study of Social Organizations with Survey Methods," *Human Organization* 17 (1958): 29.

12. "Structural Effects," *American Sociological Review* 25 (Apr. 1960): 178–92.

13. *Political Man* (Garden City, N.Y., 1960), ch. 11.

14. An excellent review of recent organizational research can be found in Wolf V. Heydebrand, "The Study of Organizations," *Social Science Information* 6 (Oct. 1967): 59–87.

15. *TVA and the Grass Roots* (Berkeley 1949).

16. "From Organization to Society: Virginia in the 17th Century," *American Journal of Sociology* 63 (Mar. 1958): 457–75.

17. "The Origins of American Politics," *Perspectives in American History*, 1 (1967): 9–80.

18. Dahrendorf, *Gesellschaft und Demokratie in Deutschland* (Munich 1966); Eckstein, *Division and Cohesion in Democracy: A Study of Norway* (Princeton 1966).

19. Alex Inkeles and Raymond Bauer, *The Soviet Citizen* (Cambridge, Mass., 1959); Thomas H. Marshall, *Class, Citizenship and Social Development* (New York 1964); Amitai Etzioni, *Political Unification* (New York 1965); S. N. Eisenstadt, *Political Systems of Empires* (New York 1963).

20. Richard L. Merritt and Stein Rokkan (eds.), *Comparing Nations—the Use of Data in Cross-National Research* (New Haven 1966).

21. *The First New Nation: The United States in Historical and Comparative Perspective* (New York 1963).

22. *Politics, Personality, and Nation Building: Burma's Search for Identity* (New Haven 1963).

23. *Relative Deprivation and Social Justice* (Berkeley 1966). Cf. S. A. Stouffer et al., *The American Soldier* (Princeton 1949).

24. Dray (ed.), *Philosophical Analysis and History* (New York 1966).

25. *Social Change in the Industrial Revolution: An Application of Theory to the British Cotton Industry, 1770–1840* (Chicago 1959).

26. Lazarsfeld [n. 3]. The introduction to the latest ed. reviews most of the panel studies carried out in recent years.

27. C. Wright Mills et al., *The Puerto Rican Journey* (New York 1950).

28. The numerous studies on diffusion of innovation among farmers provide suggestive comparisons with historical literature. For summary and bibliography, see Charles F. and Zona Loomis, "Rural Sociology," ed. Lazarsfeld et al., *The Uses of Sociology* (New York 1967): 655.

29. The technique of this kind of decision analysis is described and discussed in Hans Zeisel, *Say it with Figures*, 4th ed. (New York 1965).

30. "American Imperialism: A Reinterpretation," *Perspectives in American History*, 1 (1967): 123–287.

31. "History and the Social Sciences," ed. Fritz Stern, *The Varieties of History* (Cleveland 1956): 364 ff.

32. *French Opinion on War and Diplomacy During the Second Empire* (Philadelphia 1954).

33. Contributors to Norman Jacobs (ed.), *Culture for the Millions* (Boston 1964), represent all possible views on this issue.

34. "An Historical Preface to the Popular Culture Debate," ed. Jacobs [n. 33]: 28.

35. Paul F. Lazarsfeld and Anthony Oberschall, "Max Weber and Empirical Social Research," *American Sociological Review* 30 (Apr. 1965): 185–99.

36. "The Obligations of the 1950 Pollster to the 1984 Historian," *Public Opinion Quarterly* 14 (Winter 1950–51): 617–38.

37. Ward, *Andrew Jackson, Symbol for an Age* (New York 1955); Meyers, *The Jacksonian Persuasion*, rev. ed. (New York 1960).

38. "Money and Party in Jacksonian America," *Political Science Quarterly* 82 (June 1967): 235–52.

39. *The Secession Conventions of the South* (Princeton 1962).

40. Genovese, *The Political Economy of Slavery* (New York 1965); Williams, *The Tragedy of American Diplomacy* (Cleveland 1959).

Chapter 3—Cohen and Kelly

1. Samuel F. Bemis, *A Diplomatic History of the United States*, 2nd ed. (New York 1942), ch. 24, esp.: 442–50.

2. Dexter Perkins, "The Department of State and American Public Opinion," ed. Gordon A. Craig and Felix Gilbert, *The Diplomats, 1919–1939* (Princeton 1953): 295.

3. Denna F. Fleming, *The United States and the World Court* (Garden City, N.Y., 1945), esp.: 129–33.

4. Thomas Bailey, *A Diplomatic History of the American People*, 7th ed. (New York 1964): 704–5.

5. *Ibid.*: 700. Bailey adds: "In response to an overwhelming public sentiment, a Senate Committee, headed by Gerald P. Nye of North Dakota, began to hold luridly publicized hearings on the munitions traffic. . . . A swelling demand rose from the public that Congress prevent the nation's entry into another conflict by prohibiting this nefarious traffic" (700–1).

6. *Ibid.*: 778.

7. A. T. Steele, *The American People and China* (New York 1966).

8. Perkins [n. 2]: 282.

9. *Ibid.*: 298–300. And, if I may be permitted to quote Perkins one last time: "Let us summarize at this point the policies of the United States with regard to peace and security as they relate to Europe. We shall have to begin by saying once again that those policies were narrowly circumscribed by public opinion" (301).

10. Sorensen, *Kennedy* (New York 1965): 739; Schlesinger, *A Thousand Days* (New York 1967): 834.

11. *The American People and Foreign Policy,* rev. ed. (New York 1960).

12. *The Political Process and Foreign Policy: The Making of the Japanese Peace Settlement* (Princeton 1957).

13. Raymond Bauer, Ithiel de Sola Pool, and Lewis A. Dexter, *American Business and Public Policy* (New York 1963); Bernard C. Cohen, "The Influence of Non-Governmental Groups on Foreign Policy-Making," *Studies in Citizen Participation in International Relations,* 2 (Boston 1959).

14. Nelson W. Polsby, *Congress and the Presidency* (Englewood Cliffs, N.J., 1964): 26.

15. [n. 10]: 509. I will take issue at a later point with the notion that public opinion "sets the boundaries within which foreign policy makers act"—a common expression repeated here by Sorensen.

16. Frank Freidel, *America in the Twentieth Century* (New York 1960): 372–73; Norman Graebner (ed.), *Ideas and Diplomacy: Readings in the Intellectual Tradition of American Foreign Policy* (New York 1964): 562–63; Dorothy Borg, *The United States and the Far Eastern Crisis of 1933–1938* (Cambridge, Mass., 1964): 387–98.

17. *The Origins of Soviet-American Diplomacy* (Princeton 1953): 39, 99.

18. *Ibid.*: 119.

19. *Ibid.*: 103, e.g.

20. [n. 7]: 219. The unidentified author is Robert Dahl, and his observation too is offered without empirical support save for a paragraph on the World Court issue drawn from a single and not overly perspicacious observer, Cordell Hull (*Congress and Foreign Policy* [New York 1950]: 54).

21. *Ibid.*: 119. I cannot imagine a less verifiable statement about public opinion than this, that it is "consciously or subconsciously taken into consideration"; not only can 'taken into consideration' mean anything at all, but 'consciously or subconsciously' means that in a practical sense the statement is incapable of being disproved.

22. *Ibid.*: 249.

23. Walter Lippmann, *Essays in the Public Philosophy* (Boston 1955).

24. *Seen from EA* (New York 1947): 256–57. Note, incidentally, the definition of public opinion used here: the mail and the press.

25. See for example, Bauer et al. [n. 13]; Warren E. Miller and Donald E. Stokes, "Constituency Influence in Congress," *American Political Science Review* 57 (Mar. 1963): 45–56.

26. [n. 12]: 4.

27. [n. 17]: 121. If one resists the notion that Roosevelt was not very good at predicting public responses, there remains the alternate possibility that the President had tremendous and unforeseen power to shape public reaction simply by exercising policy initiative.

28. Zbigniew Brzezinski and Samuel P. Huntington, *Political Power: USA/USSR* (New York 1965): 217.

29. *The Fifteen Weeks* (New York 1955).

30. "American Public Opinion and U.S. Foreign Policy," *U.S. Dept. of State Bulletin* (Nov. 30, 1959).

31. [n. 10]: 509 and *passim*.

32. "Middle Western Newspapers and the Spanish-American War, 1895–1898," *Mississippi Valley Historical Review* 26 (Mar. 1940): 523–34.

33. [n. 16]: 369–98.

34. "Bismarck and the End of Classical Diplomacy," *Measure* 2 (Fall 1958): 376–85.

35. *The World War and American Isolation, 1914–1917* (Cambridge, Mass., 1959).

Chapter 4—Isaacs and Theoharis

1. *The Tragedy of the Chinese Revolution* (London 1938).

2. (Cambridge, Mass., 1958); pub. also as *Images of Asia* (New York 1962).

3. (New York 1931).

4. (Cornwall, N.Y., 1927).

5. Williams, *The Middle Kingdom* (New York 1883); Latourette, *The Development of China* (Boston 1917), *The History of the Early Relations Between the United States and China, 1784–1844* (New Haven 1917), *The Development of Japan* (New York 1926).

6. Emory S. Bogardus, *Immigration and Race Attitudes* (New York 1928): 25, 27–28, 74, 161.

7. My *Images of Asia* [n. 2]: 47–48.

8. Williams, *A History of the Negro Troops in the War of the Rebellion, 1861–1865* (New York 1888); Logan, *The Negro in American Life and Thought: The Nadir, 1877–1901* (New York 1954), *The Diplomatic Relations of the United States with Haiti, 1776–1891* (Chapel Hill 1941); Franklin, *From Slavery to Freedom* (New York 1947), *The Free Negro in North Carolina, 1790–1866* (Chapel Hill 1943), *Reconstruction* (Chicago 1961).

9. (Madison 1964).

10. *Theodore Roosevelt and the Rise of America to World Power* (New York 1962): 222.

11. Joseph W. Stilwell, *The Stilwell Papers* (New York 1948): 251–52.

Chapter 5—Marx and Lurie

1. Among those scholars often identified with this phase of the movement are Daniel Aaron, Allan Guttmann, R. W. B. Lewis, Charles Sanford, Henry Nash Smith, Alan Trachtenberg, and John William Ward. I should say that I am a wholly unauthorized spokesman for this wholly unorganized group.

2. Originally pub. in *American Quarterly* 9 (Summer 1957); reprinted in Joseph J. Kwiat and Mary C. Turpie (eds.), *Studies in American Culture* (Minneapolis 1960), which contains several essays that discuss or exemplify the methods of American Studies. A somewhat similar collection, ed. Marshall W. Fishwick, is *American Studies in Transition* (Philadelphia 1964).

3. Although Smith does not endorse a scientific definition of method, neither does he distinguish between the scientific and humanistic methods.

4. Harold D. Lasswell, Daniel Lerner, and Ithiel de Sola Pool, *The Comparative Study of Symbols* (Stanford 1952): 32–33.

5. "The Emergence of American Nationalism: A Quantitative Approach," *American Quarterly* 17 (Summer 1965): 321.

6. Kwiat and Turpie [n. 2]: 3.

7. The method of American Studies, in its interdisciplinary character, is comparable to the method ascribed by Lewis Mumford to the scholar who is a "generalist," that is, one whose special office is "that of bringing together widely separated fields, prudently fenced in by specialists, into a larger common area. . . . Only by forfeiting the detail can the over-all pattern be seen, though once that pattern is visible new details . . . may become visible. The generalist's competence lies not in unearthing new evidence but in putting together authentic fragments that are accidentally, or sometimes arbitrarily, separated, because specialists tend to abide too rigorously by a gentleman's agreement not to invade each other's territory." Although here Mumford is talking about the generalist in the field of prehistory, his definition is remarkably applicable to the aims of American Studies. For a fuller discussion, see *The Myth of the Machine* (New York 1966): 16–22.

8. "Truth and Politics," *New Yorker* (Feb. 25, 1967): 52.

9. The concept of literary "power" here refers to the inherent capacity of a work to generate the emotional and intellectual response of its readers. In recent years, largely as a result of the accomplishments and prestige of contextual scholars, this criterion has replaced the older academic standard, namely, that the value of a literary work depends upon its usefulness as an historical document. In effect this meant that the work was considered to be important to the degree that it was a source of knowledge about some body of extra-literary experience, such as the history of a language, the social life of a nation, or the "spirit of the age." Although the concept of literary power would seem at first glance to be ahistorical, it provides a more reliable and useful measure of historical significance than the older, relatively superficial test of representational value. In the method being described here, therefore, this key doctrine of the allegedly anti-historical "new criticism" is being incorporated into the essentially historical enterprise of American Studies.

10. Richard L. Merritt, "The Representational Model in Cross-National Content-Analysis," ed. Joseph L. Bernd, *Mathematical Applications in Political Science*, 2 (Dallas 1966): 46, 45.

11. In what follows I am describing the approach used in writing *The Machine in the Garden, Technology and the Pastoral Ideal in America* (New York 1964).

12. To improve the quality of the sociological model would seem to be the only way of meeting the criticism of the method raised by Alan Trachtenberg. In reviewing *The Machine in the Garden*, he says that the book "tends to oversimplify what was occurring outside of consciousness, 'out there' in society. [The] treatment of the dialectic within history is not as strong nor as convincing as [the] treatment of the contradictions within consciousness." Although I would substitute the terms "culture" and "social structure" for Trachtenberg's "consciousness" and "history" (or "society"), I agree with him about the inherent weakness of the method in dealing with the unverbalized, collective, institutional aspect of past behavior. For his penetrating argument, see *Nation* (July 19, 1965).

13. Charles Sanford has correctly criticized the original account of this pastoral strain in American thought for its inadequate emphasis upon the influence of Protestant evangelicism. See his review of *The Machine in the Garden* in *American Quarterly* 17 (Summer 1965).

14. See for example, Richard Hofstadter, *The Age of Reform: From Bryan to F.D.R.* (New York 1960); R. W. B. Lewis, *The American Adam: Innocence, Tragedy, and Tradition in the Nineteenth Century* (Chicago 1955); Marvin Meyers, *The Jacksonian Persuasion: Politics and Belief* (New York 1960); Charles Sanford, *The Quest for Paradise: Europe and the American Moral Imagination* (Urbana 1961); Henry N. Smith, *Virgin Land: The American West as Symbol and Myth* (Cambridge, Mass., 1950).

15. Higham made this contribution at an Arden House conference sponsored by the American Council of Learned Societies in Oct. 1960. Charles Barker and Ray Allen Billington were its organizers, and I served as executive secretary. Its purpose was to encourage the American Studies movement, to develop some sort of viable methodology, and to make it more responsive to the findings of history and other relevant social sciences. It should be stated in this context that Higham, Billington, Lurie, Hofstadter, Boorstin, Spiller, Nye, Ward, Hartz, Smith, Barker, White, and others who participated, were an informal group which shared an informal methodology.

16. This paper was delivered as the other principal address at the Arden House conference. It was read in Jones's absence; some people have wondered whether this was caused by fear of the American Studies movement, but others discount this theory and ascribe it to a bad cold.

17. This is generally referred to as "Lurie's Law No. 2."

18. I refer specifically to such books as Russel B. Nye's study of George Bancroft; Ray Billington's *The Protestant Crusade,* and his studies of the westward movement and Frederick Jackson Turner; John Hope Franklin's *From Slavery to Freedom;* Robert Spiller et al., *The Literary History of the United States;* Daniel Aaron's *Men of Good Hope* and *Writers on the Left;* Ernest Samuel's magnificent studies of Henry Adams; John Higham's *Strangers in the Land* and his history of American historical writing; as well as the already well known works of Henry Nash Smith, John William Ward, and of course, Marx himself. Significantly too, some excellent works embodying the American Studies approach (which I take to mean an essential catholicism as regards sources and insights) have been written by people who have little, if anything, to do with the organizational aspects of the movement; namely, the many distinguished works of Howard Mumford Jones and the late Perry Miller, and such recent volumes as Winthrop Jordan's *White Over Black,* Corinne Lathrop Gilb's *Hidden Hierarchies,* Thomas G. Manning's *Government in Science,* Stanley Elkins' *Slavery,* and David Brion Davis' *The Problem of Slavery in American Culture.*

Chapter 6—Merritt and Higham

I am indebted to my wife Anna J. Merritt for invaluable assistance at every point in the formulation of the research design; to Peter Melcher of the Free University of Berlin, whose creative suggestions and conscientious coding enabled the design to be realized; and to the Stimson Fund of Yale University, which provided financial support for the project. It was completed while I was Fulbright research scholar at the Otto-Suhr-Institut of the Free University of Berlin. (R.L.M.)

1. On political socialization, see Charles E. Merriam, *The Making of Citizens: A Comparative Study of Methods of Civic Training* (Chicago 1931); Herbert H. Hyman, *Political Socialization: A Study in the Psychology of Political Behavior* (Glencoe 1959); Fred I. Greenstein, *Children and Politics* (New Haven 1965); Roberta Sigel (issue ed.), "Political Socialization: Its Role in the Political Process," *Annals of the American Academy of Political and Social Science,* No. 361 (Sept. 1965); and their bibliographies.

2. On education in Germany, see Paul Kosok, *Modern Germany: A Study of Conflicting Loyalties* (Chicago 1933); Helen Liddell (ed.), *Education in Occupied Germany* (Paris 1949); Andreas Flitner, *Die politische Erziehung in Deutschland* (Tübingen 1957); Walter Stahl, *Education for Democracy in West Germany: Achievements, Shortcomings, Prospects* (New York 1961); Theodore Huebener, *The Schools of West Germany: A Study of German Elementary and Secondary Schools* (New York 1962); Hans J. Gamm, *Führung und Verführung: Pädagogik des Nationalsozialismus* (Munich 1964); Gerhard Möbus, *Unterwerfung durch Erziehung: Zur politischen Pädagogik im sowjetisch besetzten Deutschland* (Mainz 1965).

3. The basic difference between open and closed political systems in this regard is that the former tend to emphasize the "spirit of free inquiry" in the educational process. It is this openness that distinguishes education from indoctrination.

4. What I have in mind is the type of study conducted by Robert C. Angell, "Social Values of Soviet and American Elites: Content Analysis of Elite Media," *Journal of Conflict Resolution* 7 (Dec. 1964): 330–85.

5. The importance of visual reinforcement through pictures and cartoons should not be underestimated. The East Berlin text contains a mid-19th century lithograph showing what is apparently a strike or lockout, with a few management personnel, workers, and policemen on the inside of a locked fence at a factory, and many workers and a couple of policemen on the outside. In adapting this picture for use on the book's cover, an artist eliminated the parity of law-enforcement officers by transforming those on the outside into workers. Thus the image is of management and the police against the workers!

6. For alternative accounts and interpretations of the Revolution of 1848, see Karl Marx, *Revolution and Counter-Revolution; or Germany in 1848*, ed. Eleanor M. Aveling (New York 1896); Kurt H. Neumann, *Die jüdische Verfälschung des Sozialismus in der Revolution von 1848* (Berlin 1939); Theodor Heuss, *1848: Werk und Erbe* (Stuttgart 1948); Rudolf Stadelmann, *Soziale und politische Geschichte der Revolution von 1848* (Munich 1948); Wilhelm Mommsen, *Grösse und Versagen des deutschen Bürgertums: Ein Beitrag zur Geschichte der Zeit 1848–1849* (Stuttgart 1949); Priscilla S. Robertson, *Revolutions of 1848: A Social History* (Princeton 1952); Veit Valentin, *1848: Chapters of German History*, tr. (1940 ed.) Ethel T. Scheffauer (Hamden, Conn., 1965); P. H. Noyes, *Organization and Revolution: Working-Class Associations in the German Revolutions of 1848–1849* (Princeton 1966).

7. Philip J. Stone, Dexter C. Dunphy, Marshall S. Smith, and Daniel M. Ogilvie, *The General Inquirer: A Computer Approach to Content Analysis* (Cambridge, Mass., 1966).

8. Ewald Horn (ed.), *Verzeichnis der an den höheren Lehranstalten Preussens eingeführten Schulbücher*, 2d ed. (Berlin 1906).

9. *Verzeichnis der genehmigten Lehrbücher für die höheren und Mittlerer Schulen: Stand 1* (Berlin, Apr. 1931): 67–73.

10. *Amtsblatt für Berlin* 16 (2 Mar. 1966): 247 f. It would also be interesting to analyze texts from the four zones of occupation during the 1945–1949 period; see *Das Deutsche Schulbuch 1945–1950: Eine bibliographische Zusammenstellung* (n.p. 1951).

11. See note 5, above.

12. In each of the examples of reconstituted assertions, both the subject and object of action are italicized; the verb form expressing the action may not always be grammatically correct.

13. The advantage of nonparametric statistics, besides the ease of their computation, is that they do not require the researcher to make strong assumptions about the parameters

(e.g., randomness) of his data. The formula for computing the Spearman rank-order correlation coefficients is

$$r_s = 1 - \frac{6\Sigma d^2}{N(N^2 - 1)}$$

where *d* is the difference between the rankings for an item in texts A and B, and *N* is the total number of items ranked. See Sidney Siegel, *Nonparametric Statistics for the Behavioral Sciences* (New York 1956): 202–13.

14. See for example, John Higham with Leonard Krieger and Felix Gilbert, *History (Humanistic Scholarship in America: The Princeton Studies,* Englewood Cliffs, N.J., 1965), esp. Gilbert's account of how this change occurred in Western Europe: 341–81.

15. *Symbols of American Community, 1735–1775* (New Haven 1966).

16. John Higham, "The Schism in American Scholarship," *American Historical Review* 72 (Oct. 1966): 1–21.

Index of Persons

Aaron, Daniel, 134, 189 n.1, 191 n.18
Adams, Henry, 136
Adams, John Quincy, 86
Adler, Kenneth P., 185 n.59
Albig, William, 183 n.26, 184 n.35
Alger, Horatio, 25
Allport, Floyd H., 18
Almond, Gabriel A., 70, 181 n.8, 182 n.21, 183 n.28, 186 n.65
Ander, Oscar F., 184 n.46
Angell, Robert C., 192 n.4
Apter, David, 185 n.60
Arendt, Hannah, 117
Arendt, Hans-Jürgen, 152
Aristotle, 132
Arndt, Ernst Moritz, 156
Auxier, George W., 80, 84
Aveling, Eleanor M., 192 n.6

Bailey, Thomas A., 17, 84, 187 n.4, 188 n.5
Bailyn, Bernard, 50, 60
Barker, Charles, 191 n.15
Barrett, Irving, 134
Bartel, Horst, 152
Bauer, Alice, 185 n.61
Bauer, Raymond A., 51, 71, 185 n.66, 186 n.19, 188 n.13, n.25
Beale, Howard K., 104
Bemis, Samuel Flagg, 187 n.1
Benedict, Ruth, 134
Benson, Lee, 45–46, 60, 61, 184 n.43
Berelson, Bernard, 185 n.50, n.51
Berlew, David, 42
Bernd, Joseph L., **185 n.54, 190 n.10**
Bigman, Stanley K., 185 n.59
Billington, Ray Allen, 191 n.15, n.18
Bismarck, Otto von, 14, 143, 145
Blaine, James G., 46
Blau, Peter, 47
Bloch, Marc, 58
Blum, Robert, 154
Blumer, J. G., 186 n.7
Bobrow, Davis, 185 n.59

Bogardus, Emory S., 100
Bonaparte, Napoleon, 88
Bonwetsch, G., 151
Boorstin, Daniel, 184 n.37, n.48, 191 n.15
Borg, Dorothy, 80, 188 n.16
Boulding, Kenneth, 184 n.37
Bradburn, Norman, 42
Breckenridge, John C., 48
Briand, Aristide, 67, 83, 107
Browder, Robert, 72–73, 78, 87
Bruckberger, Raymond L., 184 n.37
Bryan, William Jennings, 46
Brzezinski, Zbigniew, 78, 189 n.28
Buchanan, William, 186 n.66
Buck, Pearl S., 26, 96, 99, 107
Burckhardt, Jacob, 57

Campbell, Angus, 183 n.33
Cannell, Charles F., 185 n.52
Canning, George, 85
Cantril, Hadley, 41, 186 n.3, n.66
Carlyle, Thomas, 57, 95
Carr, Edward Hallett, 95
Carranza, Venustiano, 23
Carroll, Eber Malcolm, 16, 20, 183 n.31
Case, Lynn M., 56, 182 n.21
Castlereagh, Viscount, 85, 87
Chamberlain, Joseph, 14
Chan, Charlie, 99
Chiang Kai-Shek, 93
Childs, Harwood L., 184 n.35
Cohen, Bernard C., 10, 15, 20, 21, 64, 65–80, 81–88, 183 n.31, 188 n.13
Coleman, James, 47
Converse, Philip, 30
Coughlin, Charles, 67
Craig, Gordon A., 181 n.8, 187 n.2
Cummings, Milton C., 184 n.37
Curti, Merle, 60
Curtin, Philip D., 103, 184 n.37

Dahl, Robert, 188 n.20
Dahrendorf, Ralf, 50, 52, 186 n.18

Melvin Small, associate professor of history, Wayne State University, did his undergraduate work at Dartmouth College and received his M.A. and Ph.D. (1965) from the University of Michigan. Professor Small is co-author of *The Wages of War, 1816–1965* (in press) and a fellow at the Center for Advanced Study in the Behavioral Sciences, Stanford, 1969–70.

Charles H. Elam edited the manuscript. This book was designed by Joanne Colman. The type face used is Granjon, designed by George W. Jones in 1924. The book is printed on S. D. Warren's Olde Style Antique and bound in Columbia Mills cloth over binder's boards. Manufactured in the United States of America.

438361